A Technique for Loving

A Technique for Loving

*Non-Violence in Indian and
Christian Traditions*

PETER D. BISHOP

SCM PRESS LTD

334 01601 0

First published 1981
by SCM Press Ltd
58 Bloomsbury Street London WC1

Photoset by Input Typesetting Ltd
and printed in Great Britain by
Richard Clay Ltd (The Chaucer Press)
Bungay

Contents

To Anne

Preface

It is difficult to imagine any matter of greater importance than the pursuit of peace. We now live in a world in which nations possess stocks of armaments capable of destroying every human being several times over. The danger of nuclear war is obvious enough, and its perils almost unthinkable. Is it conceivable that the religions of the world should have anything helpful and constructive to say on the great issues of peace and war? Some religious teaching about violence and non-violence may appear to be hopelessly impracticable. The injunction to turn the other cheek and the teaching about absolute *ahimsa* found in some Eastern religions may seem to be appropriate ideals for the holy few but quite inadequate for those of us who have to go on living in a harsh and violent world.

In the West the Christian attitude to war has been expressed in the careful formulations of the just war doctrine, a theoretical approach adhered to in principle, if not always in practice, for many centuries. But it is now clear that the just war theory became untenable during the 1940s. With the deliberate mass-bombing of civilian targets as a policy for terrorizing populations during the Second World War, and with the advent of nuclear weapons, the whole theory of the just war is in shreds. It is evident that mass-bombing of civilians and nuclear war amount in moral terms to mass-murder. So what are we to do? Should we refuse all participation in war and become pacifists? Or should we forget our consciences and become parties to mass-murder?

The just war doctrine was the product of Christian thought, formulated in the cultural isolation of Western Europe. One of the benefits of studying religion today is that we no longer need to be confined to the study of one religious tradition. Indeed, if we know only one religion, our religious understanding is likely to be not only partial but inadequate. An examination of different religious traditions in their attitudes to conflict and violence offers the possibility of a reformulation of traditional attitudes to war and peace. And that is the starting-point for this book.

After a survey of Christian and Indian attitudes to war and peace, violence and non-violence, the book concentrates upon a study of the uses made of techniques of non-violent resistance by Mahatma Gandhi and Martin Luther King Jr. In the course of this study there emerges, I believe, the basis for a programme of action which offers the person of conscience a way out of the paralysis engendered by what appears to be an impossible choice between immoral mass warfare and ineffective pacifism.

I gladly acknowledge much help received whilst researching and writing this book. A grant from the John Finch Travelling Bursary, supplemented by funds from Brighton Polytechnic, enabled me to visit India (a country in which I had lived happily for seven years) in order to study material related to Gandhiji. I am grateful to the staff of the Gandhi Memorial Museum and Library, Delhi, the Nehru Memorial Museum and Library and the National Archives of India, New Delhi, for their courtesy and assistance in that part of the work. In 1980 the British Academy gave me an award from their Small Grants Research Fund in the Humanities which enabled me to visit the United States of America and meet people who knew Martin Luther King Jr or who worked in the civil rights movement in which he was involved. That visit introduced me to a number of hospitable and kindly people who greatly helped my understanding of Martin King and the context in which he worked.

Peter D. Bishop

I

Religion and Violence

For centuries adherents of several of the major religions have claimed religious authority for attitudes of peace and non-violence. Many have claimed that the authority and inspiration of religion is a necessary part of the true art of loving one's neighbour. Christians have looked admiringly at the Sermon on the Mount and the example of sacrificial suffering which is found in Jesus Christ. Hindus have maintained that the doctrine of *ahimsa*, of not harming people and other forms of life, is an essential ingredient of their tradition. Buddhists have emphasized the continuing importance of a form of *ahimsa* in their religion and point to the importance of Buddhist ideas in influencing Hinduism. Buddhists who have been concerned in recent years with the exposition of their faith as a missionary religion have claimed the peaceful nature of Buddhism as one of its most attractive elements. In comparatively recent times several notable apologists for religion have identified 'reverence for life' as a fundamental part of what religion conveys to those who seek to find and embrace its truth.

Yet another, and gloomier, side of the picture of religions as agents of pacific attitudes is all too clear. Devotion to the cause of religion has been the cause of violence and bloodshed throughout the long history of religions. It is an unfortunate fact that devotion to a noble cause and blind bigotry can all too easily be part of the same religious experience. Suspicion, condemnation, and even hatred of those who do not share one's own religious belief is an unhappy but persistent feature of religious life.

At certain times and places in its history Islam has adopted Jihad, or holy war, as a legitimate method of spreading the faith of submission to Allah. Christian history includes the tragic and senseless confrontation with Islam which has been romanticized in the story of the Crusades but which is in fact an episode reflecting little credit and much shame on the church. Wars of conscience have been the cause of immense suffering in Christian Europe, so that it may appear that the very worst and most barbarous of conflicts are likely to be those which are fought for the very best of motives.

Nor is the record of violence restricted to the Middle East and the West. Eastern religions have had some success this century in presenting themselves as vehicles of tolerance and peace. But the history of Hinduism, for example, includes many instances of repression and violent opposition to those who appeared to threaten the religious and social structures of Hindu life. Many scholars would regard the violent opposition of Hinduism as an important factor in accounting for the decline of Buddhism in the country of its birth, although the *coup de grace* was administered to the Buddhists by Muslim invaders of India. The most popular of Hindu scriptures, the *Bhagavad Gita*, is regarded by some (I believe rightly) as as an important text in the struggle against Buddhism. One may feel sympathy in their later history for the gentle Hindus, who were overwhelmed by the invading Muslims, but in truth must acknowledge that the opposition of the Rajputs and of the Vijayanagar Empire was never intended to be con- ducted in the gentle tones of peaceful persuasion.

This is ancient history, and religions have been reformed in more recent times. Yet religious factors continue to intrude into conflicts. The tragic affairs of Northern Ireland clearly are not all to be explained in terms of Protestant versus Catholic, in spite of the media's addiction to the use of those convenient labels. Church leaders on both sides have urged moderation on their 'followers' and tried hard to bring about reconciliation. In spite of their efforts, however, it has to be acknowledged that many years of religious bigotry, zealously fostered by churches and by the edu- cational system, have contributed to the present sad situation.

Are violence and bigotry, then, essentially bound up with religion? It is the contention of this book that they are not. And furthermore, that a sane and enlightened religious commitment can be a powerful force for peace.

Religious teaching, in Christianity and in several Eastern religions, contains important guidance on basically non-violent responses to situations of conflict. The fact that adherents of these religions have not always been successful in applying this aspect of their faith to social life does not of itself nullify the teaching.

Of special interest is the fact that techniques of non-violent resistance, based upon religious teaching, have been employed with some success during the last fifty years. They have been employed to overcome injustice and to gain political ends. The achievements of Mahatma Gandhi, the Hindu who was the foremost leader of the Indian Independence movement from 1920 until 1947, are extremely well known, and his deeply religious character and simple style of life have won him deep respect throughout the world. Gandhiji insisted upon the necessity of a non-violent approach to politics as a way of relating means to ends, and of pursuing truth in social and political spheres. Gandhi's non-violence was fed by several sources: traditional Jaina and Hindu teaching on *ahimsa*; the model of renunciation, common to Jainism, Hinduism, and Buddhism; the writings of such Westerners as Ruskin, Thoreau, and Tolstoy; and, by no means least, the Sermon on the Mount.

To this Hindu who borrowed from the West there later came a Westerner who found inspiration in Mahatma Gandhi's technique, re-baptized his method into a Christian context, and led a powerful non-violent campaign in the United States. Martin Luther King's use of the Gandhian method presents a fascinating example of the exchange of understanding and insights across religious and cultural barriers which is so important a feature of our time.

In the pages that follow there is an interpretation of Christian attitudes to non-violence and war, and an exposition of Jaina, Hindu, and Buddhist teaching on *ahimsa*. There follows an account of the way in which Mahatma Gandhi used and adapted these traditions, and a critical evaluation of the theology which lay behind his method. Attention then turns to Martin Luther King, and the similarities and contrasts with Gandhi which appeared in his campaigns.

Much has been written and spoken in Christian circles recently about the need to accept violent methods of change, and the new genre of books on the 'theology of liberation' includes contributions by writers who regard non-violence as weak and ineffective in the struggle for justice. In the light of this development an attempt is made to outline a Christian theology of non-violent action which takes account of the insights offered by other great religious traditions, but which finally focuses upon the particular contribution to be made by Christian thought, faith, and action, and suggests how such a theology might be applied in contemporary situations.

2

Christian Attitudes to Violence

Christian traditions and Christian scriptures reveal ambivalent attitudes to violence. Christians vary in the degree of authority they attribute to the Old Testament, but however interpreted, the Hebrew scriptures remain part of the Christian tradition, and some account must be taken of them in making a theological judgment on such a matter as Christian attitudes to violence. Some Christians have justified warlike attitudes by the use of Old Testament texts, and taken as a whole, the Old Testament provides little comfort for apostles of non-violence.

In its treatment of the early history of the people of Israel the Old Testament regards warfare as a powerful weapon used by Yahweh to discomfort the enemies of Israel and to establish the Chosen People in their Promised Land.[1] Parts of the narrative suggest that not only victory but the complete annihilation of the enemy, women, children, and property included, was thought to be pleasing to Yahweh.[2] The later experience of the people of Israel led to more subtle views, and especially to a moving interpretation of their own sufferings and defeats as part of the outworking of the will of God.

By the end of the Old Testament period a variety of views about the place of violence in their past history and future destiny was held by the Jewish people. Some looked expectantly for a Messiah who would be a successful warrior-prince, lead his people to victory, throw off the yoke of foreign domination, and establish Israel as the most powerful of the nations. Others related their nation's past sufferings to their own experiences, and thought of Jewish destiny in terms suggested by Isaiah's description of the 'suffering servant'. But on balance the Old Testament would appear to give greater support to those who would wage holy war

4

than to those who wished to beat their swords into ploughshares.

The history of the Jewish people from 200 BC to 120 CE suggests that in this period, framing the life of Jesus of Nazareth, the advocates of violent revolution commanded strong support among the Jewish people. The successful Maccabaean revolt was regarded as a great event, and its memory cherished as an example of what proud patriots could achieve long after their hard-won independence had vanished beneath the imposition of Roman rule.[3]

In the period of which the Gospel writers tell, the party of the Zealots commanded wide attention and an enthusiastic following.[4] The Zealots were committed to the overthrow of foreign rule by violent means. In aspiration and method they were similar to the modern guerrilla fighters, and parallels could be drawn between their approach and that of such twentieth-century figures as Ché Guavara, Camilo Torres, and a host of African nationalists who see in violent revolution their chief hope of salvation.

Recent research and archaeological work at Masada, where the Zealots led a last stand against the Romans in 73 CE, has led to a reassessment of the role of the Zealots. It is now recognized that their movement had an essentially religious basis, and was not simply an expression of Jewish nationalism but was concerned with the defence and re-establishment of the Torah for genuinely religious reasons. Nevertheless, the methods of the Zealots were clearly those of strong and vigorous military opposition, whether expressed in the attrition of guerrilla warfare or in the pitched battle of Masada.

A question that intrigues students of early Christianity is, to what extent were Jesus and his followers connected with the Zealots? There was at least one Zealot among his band of close disciples. Matthew and Mark list among the disciples 'Simon the Cananaean'; Luke calls the same person 'Simon the Zealot', and in doing so is simply giving the Greek word for the Aramaic of Matthew and Mark.[5] 'Cananaean' does not mean that Simon came from a place called Cana; the Aramaic *qan'ana* means 'zealot'. Luke repeats the description 'Simon the Zealot' in Acts 1. Then there is the position of Judas Iscariot. What does the word 'Iscariot' mean? Many scholars find the likeliest explanation in the suggestion that it derives from 'Sicarii',[6] a word which means 'dagger-men', or assassins, and was used of an extremist group among the Zealots. It is an attractive interpretation of the character of Judas to assume that he was not a pre-determined traitor selling his soul for a few pieces of silver, but an ardent Jewish

nationalist, committed to violent revolution, and believing that
Jesus must declare himself as a political and military Messiah if
he were to be faced with arrest and trial.

The existence of some Zealot influence among the followers of
Jesus no doubt coloured the attitude of the authorities to him.
Recent comment on the trial of Jesus has drawn attention to a
number of curiosities in the record contained in the Gospels.[7]
Why did the Jews need to send Jesus to Pilate when their own
courts had the power to pass and carry out the sentence of death
for blasphemy? Why should the Roman authorities have been so
concerned about a man who, according to the Sanhedrin, seemed
to be just another Jewish eccentric, claiming to be the Messiah or
the Son of God? And why should Pilate, whom other records
suggest to have been a ruthless and determined man, have released someone called Barabbas, a known revolutionary, and executed Jesus instead? Matters of specialist New Testament
scholarship are beyond the scope of this book, and the issues are
complex. But a sufficient case does seem to have been made at
least to make us look sympathetically at the suggestion that in
writing down the Gospel records of these matters the early church
was influenced by its own delicate relationships with Judaism and
the Roman authorities. With regard to Judaism, the church was
anxious to establish itself as the new Israel and Jesus as the true
Messiah over against the claims of the Jews. That the *Jews* were
the ones who betrayed Jesus and handed him over to be executed
fitted in very well with the notion of an apostate Israel whose
place had now been taken by a new chosen people. That theme
recurs many times in the history of the church, and is part of the
tragedy of Christian antisemitism. With regard to the Romans, it
was obviously difficult for Christians in the Roman Empire during
the sensitive years just before and immediately after the Jewish
revolt of 66–70 CE to circulate material which blamed the Roman
authorities for executing their Lord, or even to acknowledge that
Jesus had been condemned by a Roman court on a charge of
treason. Hence the carefully tailored accounts which suggested
that it was the Jews who had been responsible for the condemnation and execution of Jesus, even though it was the Romans
who had carried out the execution.

The strength of Zealot influence upon Jesus and his disciples
cannot be known with any real degree of accuracy, but some
scholars have maintained that it was a very important factor in
the events of which the Gospels tell. S. G. F. Brandon has argued
that the movement around Jesus was basically one of revolution-

aries committed to the violent overthrow of Roman rule. Jesus, he maintains, was regarded as the Messianic leader of such a nationalistic movement, and his arrest, trial, and crucifixion are to be understood in this light.

Popular religious writing has taken up this theme, and the colourful pen of Colin Morris has used Brandon's argument to suggest to the 'unyoung, uncoloured, unpoor' of the world that their less privileged brethren would be justified in rising against them in armed conflict.[8]

The argument that Jesus himself was a Zealot seems to me to be not proven. That there were Zealots among his immediate followers is not in doubt. That Judas was motivated by a desire to spur Jesus into action, believing him to be a Messiah who would give his leadership to armed revolt, appears most likely. But the Gospel record also indicates continual misunderstanding between Jesus and his followers. Reiterated warnings that 'the Son of man must suffer . . . and be killed'[9] were misunderstood by his followers, who appear to have been perplexed by the notion of a Messiah who could willingly contemplate death and defeat. Those who embark upon armed revolt must be prepared for violent opposition and, therefore, for the possibility of death. But it would be a curious general who approached a conflict in the certainty of his own death and the scattering of his followers. Is it not more likely that misunderstandings between Jesus and his disciples were caused by genuine differences? The disciples naturally accepted the popular assumption that the Messiah would come clothed in power; Jesus, on the other hand, appears to have applied to himself the poignant description of the Suffering Servant provided by the prophet Isaiah. The latter part of the Gospel record is dominated by the attempts of Jesus to make his followers understand what he was doing, and why. The Gospels suggest that he was unsuccessful in the attempt, and that only after the crucifixion and resurrection did the disciples begin to understand.

Of course, we can read the Gospel record only through the eyes of the early church, in which the sayings and doings of Jesus and his followers were preserved, repeated, enshrined in liturgy, and only after thirty years and more written down. After the fall of Jerusalem in 70 CE, realists within the Christian Church had little option but to spiritualize the message they had received. But then to assume that Jesus himself was committed to the idea (a misguided idea, as it turned out) that the way to freedom and liberty for his people was through violent revolution appears to me to be spurious.

That the teaching of Jesus pointed in a different direction seems a more likely interpretation.

Quoting biblical texts is likely to be an unrewarding pastime unless the whole tenor of biblical teaching is taken into account, and individual texts related to overall themes. The support of the New Testament has been adduced for warlike attitudes on the part of Christians, and some modern interpretations, as we have seen, would read from the Gospel record an assumption that violent revolution in a just cause is directly sanctioned by the example of Jesus. Others have argued an uncompromising pacifist view on the basis of the New Testament. Neither of these positions is taken here.

There can be little doubt, however, of the importance of the New Testament and the records of the Gospels for Christian interpretations of ethical issues. For the Christian the Old Testament is fulfilled, and sometimes abrogated, by the New. The apparently vengeful passages of the Old Testament should not stand as an authority of equal weight with the New Testament for the orthodox Christian. For orthodoxy accepts that the 'Word of God' is Jesus Christ himself, and not a set of scriptures. The whole of the Bible, including the Old Testament, is to be judged, so far as it may be possible, by the light shed upon its pages by the life and teaching of Jesus.

What, then, of the New Testament?

To look first at the Sermon on the Mount is to look at a section of the New Testament which has been quoted often either to support non-violent attitudes on the part of Christians or to cast scorn on the impracticability of such standards. This section of the New Testament has been regarded by many non-Christians, as well as by Christians, as containing the quintessence of the ethical teaching of Jesus; and so, some would say, the real core of his message.

On response to violence, the Sermon on the Mount seems to be clear enough:

You have heard that it was said, 'An eye for an eye and a tooth for a tooth.' But I say to you, Do not resist one who is evil. But if anyone strikes you on the right cheek, turn to him the other also; and if any one would sue you and take your coat, let him have your cloak as well; and if any one forces you to go one mile, go with him two miles. Give to him who begs from you, and do not refuse him who would borrow from you.

You have heard that it was said, 'You shall love your neigh-

bour and hate your enemy.' But I say to you, Love your enemies
and pray for those who persecute you, so that you may be sons
of your Father who is in heaven; for he makes his sun rise on
the evil and on the good, and sends rain on the just and on the
unjust. For if you love those who love you, what reward have
you?[10]

This does not have about it the ring of an oration delivered by a
guerrilla leader on the eve of sending his men into battle. Nor
does it contain much immediately useful advice for a member of
the armed forces who is about to face foreign foe or civil insur-
rection. Nevertheless, before taking it to be a totally pacifist text,
some qualification is required.

The Sermon on the Mount, like other ethical teaching of Jesus,
ought not to be regarded simply as a new law. It surely was not
intended as a direct substitute for the Mosaic Law and the scribal
interpretations which supplemented that Law. The teaching of
Jesus was of a different kind. Jesus took as his starting point that
portion of the Law which adjured men to love God and love their
neighbour to the utmost. He then gave, in words and by example,
illustrations of what it might mean to love God and love one's
neighbour. An example of this approach outside the Sermon on
the Mount is to be found in the story of the Good Samaritan. The
lawyer's question, 'And who is my neighbour?' was presumably
asked in expectation of a clear definition. But it was not answered
directly. Instead, Jesus told the story of the Good Samaritan. It
was an illustration of what it might mean to be a good neighbour
on the bandit-infested road between Jerusalem and Jericho and
also, shocking as it must have appeared to those who first heard
the story, it cast a despised schismatic and foreigner in the role of
the 'good neighbour'. It was a powerful reply. But it was far from
being a clear definition that could be followed in any situation.

The same kind of approach can be seen in direct sayings of
Jesus. He frequently used picturesque expressions which were not
meant to be taken literally, but which vividly illuminated his point.
So, stressing the unique worth of each individual in the sight of
God, he is reported to have said: 'Why, even the hairs of your
head are all numbered.'[11] Only a lunatic, on reading such words,
would thrust his head under a microscope and invite a friend to
look for the heavenly branding in his hair. In such cases we
understand the metaphorical nature of the words.

Similarly, in the Sermon on the Mount, Jesus used vivid sayings in order to suggest the radical demands involved in loving God and neighbour. So we read:

> If your right eye causes you to sin, pluck it out and throw it away; it is better that you lose one of your members than that your whole body be thrown into hell. And if your right hand causes you to sin, cut it off and throw it away . . .[12]

Yet we do not presume on this account that the ideal Christian is likely to have only one eye and one hand. We appreciate the picturesque nature of the speech. Gradually, however, a picture does emerge. Repeated sayings of this kind, stories such as the Good Samaritan, and loving action on the part of Jesus, all add up to a coherent pattern in which we can discern what Jesus meant by 'love God and love your neighbour'. In the celebrated phrase of I. T. Ramsey, 'the penny drops, the light dawns', and we see where the teaching and example is leading.

However, this does present difficulties. If not every saying is to be taken literally, how are we to distinguish the illustration from the command? The answer, surely, lies in appreciating that the ethical teaching of Jesus is illustration, and not command. The difficult task of applying the spirit of his teaching to our own situation is left to us.

The Sermon on the Mount, then, must be set alongside the rest of the teaching of Jesus, read in the light of the total example of his life, and then applied to the world in which we live. And although they do not have the nature of law, the sayings about going an extra mile, and loving your enemy as well as your neighbour, do convey to us very powerfully an attitude towards situations of actual or potential violent confrontation which is distinct and effective. They are not law, for love cannot be prescribed by law. Rather, they suggest a technique for loving which is complemented by other parts of the New Testament.

To move from a reading of the Gospels to the Epistles of Paul is to enter a new and different atmosphere, and some scholars have maintained that Paul invented a system fundamentally different from the teaching of Jesus of Nazareth. Paul's writings set out the doctrine of the cosmic Christ and pay much attention to the thorny question of relationships between Christianity and Judaism. Yet Paul is also very clear about what he calls 'grace' – the undeserved love of God for men, and the human response of a certain kind of love which he saw to be sacrificial, compassionate, and deeply concerned for the good of others. When he reflected upon the gifts which were regarded as being given to the church by the Holy Spirit, he concluded that the most important was love. This he saw to be more important than the curious but exciting phenomena of 'speaking in tongues', and more important even than the vital gift of faith. Paul defined love as an attitude towards others compounded of patience, kindness, and humility; an attitude which actively seeks the good of another person rather than pursuing self-interest. The ethic involved in the exercise of such love is suggested in Romans 12:

> Care as much about each other as about yourselves . . .
> Never pay back evil for evil . . .
> Do not let evil conquer you, but use good to defeat evil.[13]

In an important New Testament passage in the First Letter of John, the character of God is summed up in terms of love and loving relationships. God is said to be known through love, so that those who love know God, and those who do not love cannot know God.

This is a distinctive element in the New Testament, asserting that God, or ultimate reality, is to be known primarily through the exercise of loving relationships rather than through law or knowledge.[14]

The New Testament reflects the understanding of the church as well as the teaching of Jesus. The interpretations, credal forms, and liturgies of the early church were part of the complex of influences working upon the records which were to become the New Testament in the very process of their being written. In studying the New Testament we are in part looking at the beliefs and practices of the Church during the formative period between 50 and 120 CE. So it is not surprising that a process of development can be seen within the New Testament. When Paul wrote the Letter to the Romans, in the late fifties of the first century, he could confidently recommend to his Christian readers a policy of obedience to the secular authorities, no doubt on the assumption that the preservation of peace and order in the Roman Empire was in the interests of the Christians.

> Every person must submit to the supreme authorities. There is no authority but by act of God, and the existing authorities are instituted by him.[15]

But by the time Revelation came to be written, perhaps in 95 or 96 CE, attitudes had changed. The state had become the fierce persecutor of the church and so could be described as a beast with ten horns and seven heads. Christians could now long for the overthrow of the Empire that once had been their protector.

But in spite of the persecutions they suffered, Christians in the early period appear to have held to the conviction that non-violent rather than violent action was the norm for believers. The New Testament does suggest an interest in the message of Christ on the part of a centurion in the Roman army; but a career in the army appears to have been a most unlikely choice for people actually converted to Christianity during the early period of Christian history. Roland Bainton asserts that 'from the end of the New Testament period to the decade AD 170–180 there is no evidence whatever of Christians in the army'.[16] Bainton's interpretation of this lack of evidence is to accept the probability that abstention from military service was taken for granted among Christians. Confirmation of this appears to come from Celsus, who reproached Christians with the possible consequences of a refusal to take up arms to defend the sovereign and the empire. To the pagan philosopher this was proof of the decadence of Christianity. But to a number of early Christian writers, pacifism appears to have been both normal and virtuous. Tertullian, Justin Martyr, and Cyprian all make comments which seem to support the view that Christians in the first two centuries were pacifists. Tertullian's celebrated saying that 'Christ in disarming Peter ungirt every soldier'[17] cannot be taken as evidence that Christians never served in the army, but certainly it is part of his argument against Christian participation in military occupations. In 197 CE he referred to the presence of Christians in the palace, the senate, the forum, and the army.[18] It is known that there were Christian soldiers in the Thundering Legion in Southern Armenia in 173, and that in the same area Christians took to arms against an emperor who attempted to enforce idolatry. But it is most likely that soldiers who were Christians were converted after their entry into the army.

Justin Martyr, writing around 160, claimed that the act of becoming a Christian changed a person's attitude to participation in military activities:

> We who were filled with war and mutual slaughter and every wickedness have each of us in all the world changed our weapons of war . . . swords into ploughs and spears into agricultural implements.[19]

Some Christian writers appear to have drawn distinctions between different kinds of military service, assuming that it was legitimate for Christians to serve in the army if such service could be restricted to ceremonial and policing activities. So the Canons of Hippolytus, written in the early third century, maintained that 'a soldier of the civil authority must be taught not to kill men, and to refuse to do so if he is commanded'.[20]

All this supports the view that for nearly three hundred years, while Christians were a despised and sometimes persecuted minority in the Roman Empire, they generally held to the belief that there is a contradiction between the profession of Christian faith and participation in warfare.[21] The teaching of Christ and the main thrust of the New Testament ethic suggested to them that acceptance of Christian faith involved the acceptance of a forgiving love which could not readily be reconciled with the demands of a military career.[22]

The position was changed by the conversion of the Emperor Constantine and the subsequent acceptance of Christianity as the principal religion of the Empire. From being a decried minority, Christians moved to being the representatives of the official religion, and so inevitably associated with the exercise of power and public authority. There was no attempt to carry into the arena of public affairs the pacifism which had seemed appropriate for a minority movement. On the whole, Christians came to accept the view that their duty to the state included a necessity to defend the authority and integrity of the empire, by military means if necessary. By the fifth century the Emperor Theodosius was able to proclaim that those polluted by pagan rites should be excluded from the army, and that only Christians should serve in it.[23]

A caveat was entered against the wholesale participation of Christians in warfare, however, by the distinction which came to be drawn between the clergy and the laity. The fourth-century theologian Eusebius of Caesarea taught that the clergy should be exempt from military service, whilst the laity should exercise the burdens of citizenship, including that of waging just wars.[24] Ambrose, bishop of Milan and a former high civil servant, extolled the virtues of the deeds of the Emperor Augustus in pacifying the empire and so providing a suitable environment for the spread of Christianity.

> The courage of soldiers who defended the Empire against Barbarians and Roman citizens from thieves was full of justice, and Ambrose prayed for the success of the imperial armies.[25]

The views of Ambrose were further developed by the great Augustine of Hippo (354–430). Towards the end of his life Augustine found it necessary to deal theologically with the problems caused by the assault on the stability and order of the Roman Empire by the barbarians. In view of this necessity it was perhaps natural that he should have advocated the participation of Christians in warfare, using the Old Testament to support his view. Two important elements in Augustine's teaching on war were, firstly the relegation of pacifism to the spheres of monks and priests, and secondly the enunciation of a doctrine of the 'just war'. A just war, according to Augustine, was one waged only because of a necessity to vindicate justice and to deliver people from war. Augustine devised a neat distinction between the inward disposition of the heart and the outward deed, thus making it possible to regard the injunction to 'turn the other cheek' as referring simply to an inward attitude which could be held even when, outwardly, one was engaged in killing the enemy. Indeed, according to Augustine an act of hostility could be performed in a spirit of charity. Augustine also declared that a soldier who killed on orders in a just war was absolved from any moral responsibility for killing.[26] Thus the theologians conveniently reconciled the consciences of Christians with the needs of the state. After the fall of the Roman Empire, Christian authorities felt bound to uphold the right of self-defence on the part of their Christian subjects.

The ideas formulated by Ambrose and Augustine continued to be influential in Christian thinking about war, and gradually they came to be applied to wars between competing groups of Christians. The eleventh century saw the development of the Truce of God, which decreed that there should be no fighting between Advent and Epiphany, between Septuagesima and the eighth day after Pentecost, or on Sundays or Fridays.[27] Opportunities for sustained violence were thus strictly limited. The Peace of God, declared at the Council of Narbonne in 1054, extended exemptions from warfare beyond the categories of monks and priests. In Christian warfare, it was said, there should be no attacks on women, pilgrims, merchants, or visitors to ecclesiastical councils.[28]

These notions of carefully controlled trials of strength between opposing parties who acknowledged the same set of rules were upset by the Crusades. The chivalrous attitudes of the Truce of God and the Peace of God were abandoned. War against the infidel was not expected to follow the same rules as war between Christians. War became regarded as a moral necessity. The church became a recruiting agent, bishops in their role as princes of the state raised and sometimes led armies, and even within the monastic orders military groups were formed. The idea that the peace of a state could rightly be defended in a just war gave way to the more dangerous view that a set of beliefs should be defended and promoted in battle.

During the period of the Crusades canon law set out more formally the Christian understanding of the just war. The *Concordia Discordantium Canonum* compiled by Gratian about 1140 began with Augustinian ideas. Military service, properly authorized, was declared to be free of moral stigma when it involved defence of property or the repelling of enemy attack.[29] But Gratian moved on from this position to one which upheld the right of Christians to avenge wrongs done to the church or Christianity by heretics and infidels.[30] Eventually the theory of the Crusades came to be elaborated to give theological justification to war against the Muslims, even when such warfare was not defensive, and it was said that whoever died fighting the infidel merited eternal salvation.[31] This justification of warfare under ecclesiastical aegis helped to remove lingering doubts among Christians about the morality of war.

Nevertheless, strict limits to what war might involve were still accepted, at least in theory. The Second Lateran Council of 1139 barred the use of crossbows, bows and arrows, and siege machines against Christians, although these fearsome weapons could be employed with good conscience against infidels and heretics.[32]

The Crusading period, therefore, added a new dimension to Christian thinking about war. Theoretically war was still the business of the layman, and the monks and clergy, commonly regarded as the 'serious Christians', were exempt from its claims. The idea that the 'just war' must be defensive in its nature was still notionally adhered to. But the Crusades introduced the idea of fighting for a cause that could not be defined in terms of territory alone. The defeat of the infidel and heretic was a matter of principle, and to wage war as a matter of principle is often more terrible and vicious than to fight for a piece of territory or a similarly recognizable advantage.[33]

The long period of the Crusades also made warfare respectable in Christian eyes by blessing it with ecclesiastical approval. In the period that followed, theologians who wrote about Christians and war were often concerned to justify what Christian princes and states were already doing, rather than to lay down prescriptions for the state to follow.

What with Augustine had started out as a problem of morality and scriptural exegesis ended up as a tool of statecraft in the hands of secular monarchs.[34]

The doctrine of the just war continued to be held throughout the mediaeval period and beyond. It provided a set of conditions against which the justice of a war and the manner of its conduct could be judged. Among the conditions of the just war were demands that it should involve no declaration of war until every means to prevent it had failed; a proportionality between the evil to be done in waging war and the good to be achieved through victory; a moral certainty that the side of justice would emerge victorious; right conduct in which the means employed should keep within the limits of justice and love; respect for the rights of neutrals and of the Christian community; and a proper declaration of war by legitimate authority.[35]

After the Reformation, the Protestant churches, who examined many ecclesiastical practices in the light of biblical teaching, appropriated the idea of the just war and applied it to their own situations. It was left to sects such as the Anabaptists and the Quakers and to small minorities among Christians to pursue the path of Christian pacifism in their attempts to return to the Christianity of the New Testament. When the pacifist attitude has been adopted by such people, it has normally been seen as an ideal to be adhered to absolutely, regardless of the situations. So pacifism has been unable to accommodate the needs of the State and has remained an option for a small minority of Christians.

In recent times, however, the apparatus of war has presented a new challenge to Christians as a whole, and has thrown into question the theory of the just war.

Can a modern war be defensive? Evidently not. The strategy of nuclear warfare depends upon the capacity to launch an offensive strike even when the cities to be defended have already been destroyed.

Is it possible to limit modern warfare to certain sections of society? Again the answer is no. Even in the pre-nuclear period of the Second World War, professedly Christian nations deliberately engaged in a pattern-bombing of enemy cities which involved the indiscriminate slaughter of men, women, and children.

The theory of the just war cannot be applied to modern warfare. For the Christian this presents a cruel dilemma. Faced by the demands of the state and of war, should the Christian abandon the Bible and centuries of Christian moral teaching? Or should he abandon the world and give up any attempt to participate in the actualities of political life?

It is a benefit of contemporary theology that the Christian can gain fresh understanding and deeper insight into his own tradition by looking not only at his own faith but also at other religions. Attitudes to violence in the Eastern religions provide fresh food for thought. Especially valuable is the amalgam of Eastern and Western ideas about non-violent resistance made by Mahatma Gandhi and adapted by Martin Luther King, Jr. There, it seems to me, are the seeds of a technique of non-violent action which can be both Christian and politically realistic.

3

Renunciation

Whilst the Semitic and Western religions were developing in the Middle East and Europe, quite different religious systems continued their growth in India and South East Asia. In India the earliest religion for which there is textual evidence is that of the Aryan invaders who entered the sub-continent between 2000 and 1500 BC. Unlike later Hindus, the Aryans did not give the impression of being a gentle pacific people. Their scriptures, the Vedas, suggest that they were a warlike group, and that impression is confirmed by archaeological evidence of the destruction they wrought among the cultivated civilization of the Indus valley. A vigorous meat-eating people who imbibed the soma juice and delighted in the arts of war, the Aryans had a life-style far removed from that of later high caste Hindus.

A change in the outlook of the Indian people occurred between 800 and 500 BC. During those centuries there arose a reflexive, philosophical religion, some of which may have survived from the time before the Aryan invasion. The Upanishads provide examples of this subtle development of Indian thought, which is concerned with such matters as the nature of 'ultimate reality', transmigration or reincarnation, and *karma*.[1] In social practice the Upanishads suggested an ideal of four stages of life which would lead the male Hindu through early years of apprenticeship to a guru, learning the scriptures and acquiring wisdom, to life as a householder with responsibilities for wife and family, to retirement from the cares of this world to live in the forest, and finally, for those who pursued the path to the end, to the life of the *sannyasi*, who had renounced all the normal pleasures and the goods of this passing world. The stages of life were an ideal, and were followed in their entirety by only a small number of people, but they defined an understanding of life in which peace and bliss were to be found, not in conquest and high living, but in an escape from the mundane activities of daily life. A change had occurred in Indian thinking which was to be of great significance.

At this, the end of the Vedic age, popular religion was dominated by sacrifice and the accompanying Brahmanical cults. Possible alternatives had appeared with the development of the wisdom of the Upanishads, although this, too, was chiefly the preserve of the Brahmins. But during the same period there also arose groups of wandering ascetics who saw in programmes of self-denial the most promising possibilities for salvation or liberation. So significant were the experiences and teachings of the wandering ascetics and the challenge to Brahmanical religion which they posed that two new religions arose out of this ferment. One, Buddhism, was to become a great world religion. The other, Jainism, was to remain a purely Indian religion with a limited following, yet exerting considerable influence upon the future development of Hinduism.

The Jaina tradition, founded around 800 BC by Parsva and reformed and revitalized by Mahavira in the sixth century BC, placed very great emphasis upon asceticism. *Ahimsa*, or non-violence, was an extremely important part of the ascetic teaching of the Jainas, and a basic element of Jaina ethical principles on which other rules of conduct were based.[2]

Jainism adhered strongly to the doctrine of *karma*, which teaches that every action has consequences, good or bad, and that all bad action must be compensated for by good deeds before salvation can be attained. According to the law of *karma*, our future is determined by our actions; we create the circumstances of future lives by the deeds we perform now. What we are now is the result of the *karma* we have accumulated during previous births. The rigorous application of *karma* in Jaina religion gave added weight to *ahimsa*. Violence would lead to bad *karma*. Not only was the killing of people prohibited and violence against the person strongly deprecated, but violence against animal life was also condemned.

So the Jainas opposed the sacrificial rites of Brahmanism, in which animals were sacrificed, and they placed great importance upon vegetarianism. The marked contrast between the religion of the Rig Veda, with its hedonistic element and its appreciation of the eating of meat and drinking of soma, and later Hinduism, with its strong emphasis upon the significance of what people eat and drink, owes much to the influence of Jaina religion.

The practice of *ahimsa* was related closely to the idea of *karma*. For example, the mercy-killing of animals was condemned on the grounds that an animal's suffering could be attributed to its own past *karma*, and that there was no way by which that *karma* could be altered by killing the animal.[3] Rebirth would occur, and *karma* would have to be worked out. The combination of a strict doctrine of *karma* and an ethic which gave the dominant place to *ahimsa* strongly reinforced vegetarianism and the development of attitudes which defined religious purity in terms of what people ate and who they ate with.[4]

Jainism inevitably produced a double standard, since the more complete application of Jaina principles was possible only for the person who withdrew from the ordinary life of the world. The monk was expected to observe five principles of conduct which involved non-violence, truthfulness, not stealing or coveting, and chastity. But in all these, the monk was to pursue the intention of the 'five vows' to as extreme a conclusion as possible. The layman, it was recognized, could only attain to a modified form of the five principles, and so was required in addition to observe a further seven precepts.[5]

A description of daily life in a Jaina household, by Eberhard Fischer and Jyotindra Jain, emphasizes that *ahimsa* dominates all the activities of the Jaina:

> The day begins by sweeping the floor softly so that insects and dust are removed unharmed. Then the water needed for the day's drinking and cooking is boiled (Svetambara) or filtered several times (Digambara).[6]

Not only are all Jainas vegetarians, but they also refrain from eating such root crops as potatoes, carrots and onions because the consumption of the root destroys the whole plant. During the rainy season green vegetables are not eaten because at that time they harbour more insects, and the destruction of insects (even by accidentally eating them!) is regarded as a violation of *ahimsa*.[7] Clearly the practice of *ahimsa* is a stringent business, even for the householder.

> Generally, orthodox Jainas avoid eating fresh vegetables and eat dried vegetables or grain products and pulses. . . Orthodox Jainas do not eat anything after sunset and some do not even drink water so that no insects, not even by chance, are consumed in the drink. Since light attracts insects, both in Jaina temples and houses lights are not kept burning till late.[8]

If the layman is so particular about *ahimsa*, what of the monk? Digambara monks tend to a greater strictness than Svetambara monks and take the renunciation of possessions to an extreme that seems astonishing to the Western observer. The Digambara monk passes through three stages which are marked by a gradual increase in the severity of asceticism and a progressive shedding of clothes. At the second stage the monk wears a loin-cloth, but in the final stage the Digambara monk goes naked.[9] In the first stage he is allowed to achieve baldness by shaving his head; in the second and third stages he has to pluck out his hair. The only possessions the monk is allowed are a water-pot and a fly-whisk. Digambara monks, however, are few in number, there being only about one hundred monks of this extreme school now in existence.

Svetambara monks and nuns do not practise nudity but are nonetheless rigorous in their attitudes to possessions and in their practice of *ahimsa*. Great care is taken (by the monks) not to kill insects, since this constitutes an infringement of *ahimsa*. Water is carefully filtered before use, as much for the protection of insects as for those who might imbibe them. And monks and nuns often wear a cloth mouthpiece in order to avoid the accidental swallowing of insects. It is the Jaina monk who inherits the tradition of sweeping the ground before him as he walks in order to avoid treading on any creature.

Perhaps the most extreme application of *ahimsa*, however, is in the prohibition against taking baths. For most Indians a daily or twice-daily bath is regarded as a necessity, an act both of hygiene and of piety. But the Jaina monks relinquish this tradition in pursuit of perfect *ahimsa*, unspoilt by the killing of the tiniest creature. For might not a bath violate the tiny forms of life that live on man? To practice *ahimsa* to this degree clearly requires a level of renunication that few other religious movements would regard as either possible or desirable.

Renunciation was taken even further by many Jaina monks when they decided that they had lived long enough and were likely through age or infirmity to become a nuisance to others. They practised a self-imposed euthanasia by extending their strict diets to their logical conclusion and starving themselves to death.[10]

It is not only the careful avoidance of harming any living creature that is demanded by the Jaina religion. Jaina ethics make much of the importance of avoiding violence in thought (*bhav-ahimsa*) as well as violence in action (*dravyahimsa*). Violence in thought not only involves the kind of murderous thoughts against which the Sermon on the Mount warns, but also any restriction of the freedom of speech or thought of another.

In the rise and pursuit of the Jaina religion, then, there were formulated in India a set of attitudes which regarded asceticism and renunciation as great virtues and encouraged the extreme application of them. Careful regulation of diet was also regarded as of great importance, and in the Jaina system the religious and moral seriousness of a person could be tested simply by noting what he would and would not eat. Underlying this was a conviction that the avoidance of harm and violence to any creature, however puny, constituted the very basis of true morality and religion.

Although Jainism remained a minority movement, and even today has only two million followers in India, its influence upon the wider Indian scene has been out of all proportion to its numerical strength. Ideas of renunciation and non-violence and of the importance of diet as an indicator of a person's place in the religious and social structures have become extremely important elements in Indian life generally, and reflect the influence of the kind of ideas so firmly expressed in Jaina religion. When one looks at the life of Mahatma Gandhi and notices the importance he placed upon *ahimsa* and renunciation and diet, one has to recognize the significance of the fact that Gandhiji was born and brought up in an area deeply influenced by Jainism.

The other movement of thought and religious and social practice which deeply influenced Hinduism was the rival religion of Buddhism. With origins which related to the teaching of the wandering ascetics who challenged Brahmanism and to social and political changes in the north India of the sixth century BC,[11] Buddhism grew from another protest movement[12] into one of the great world religions. For several centuries it was a powerful force for change in India before being driven from the land of its birth to flourish in countries to the north, east, and south of India.[13]

Unlike Hinduism, Buddhism is and always has been a missionary religion, and the early preachers of Buddha *dhamma* travelled vast distances to spread their faith. But one of the proud claims of Buddhists is that their religion was never spread by violent means. Unlike the other great missionary religions of Christianity and Islam, gentle Buddhism claims never to have converted by the sword or the use of naked political power. Certainly Buddhism has acquired a reputation, which on the whole is well deserved, as a pacific religion. The missionary strategy of Buddhism in modern times has made much of the claim that it is the great religion of peace. When, after the Second World War, Buddhists in Śri Lanka launched a programme of missionary outreach to West Germany, it was partly with the idea that Buddhism would have a special contribution to make to a war-stricken land.

Buddhist teaching has always placed considerable emphasis upon non-violence, and by this emphasis it has made its own contribution to the Indian understanding of *ahimsa*. Early Buddhism formulated ethical prescriptions for monks and laymen. Laymen were expected to observe five vows: to abstain from violence, theft, lying, the use of alcohol, and illicit sexual relationships.[14] In addition they were encouraged to support the monks, or *bhikkhus*, and to tread the Noble Eightfold Path, which in Buddhist teaching provides the means of escape from the trap of impermanence and suffering and points towards Nirvana. The Eightfold Path includes injunctions to cultivate such qualities as unselfishness, generosity, and compassion. It encourages Buddhists to engage in right action, which is understood to include abstinence from killing, stealing, and drinking intoxicants. The Path also stresses the importance of the way in which a Buddhist earns his living. He should seek a means of livelihood that is conducive to spiritual growth, and avoid occupations that would involve him in breaking the precepts. So the good Buddhist should not, for example, engage in such commerce as the arms trade, nor trade in animals for slaughter, nor sell intoxicating drinks. Although the ideal Buddhist is the *bhikkhu*, the layman is encouraged to pay serious attention to *ahimsa*. And whilst Buddhism does not have an unblemished record of non-violence, it does appear to have achieved considerable success in inculcating attitudes of peaceful co-operation in its followers.[15]

Rabindranath Tagore, not himself a Buddhist, described Buddhism as 'the elimination of all limits of love'.[16] The name given to the Buddhist monk was *bhikkhu*, a word which means 'one who shares'. And the idea of encouraging co-operation and peaceful relations between people by making them interdependent has been expressed in the Buddhist system in the Sangha. From its inception Buddhism was concerned not just with individual salvation but also with a social expression of Buddhist ideals. The Sangha provided a community into which all *bhikkhus* were received regardless of caste, and in which they shared both spiritual experiences and physical resources. The Buddhist lay people were encouraged to participate in the lives of the *bhikkhus* by providing support for the Sangha. In return, they could expect guidance and inspiration from the monks. The *bhikkhu* exemplified the ideal of an ascetic, celibate, and non-violent life in which the layman could not fully share but which he could admire and emulate so far as his circumstances allowed.[17] Among the ideals which the *bhikkhus* were expected to exemplify more fully than the laymen was – and is – *ahimsa*. In a basic Buddhist text, the *Anguttara Nikaya*, it is written:

> As long as they live, the Arahants . . . are abstainers from the slaying of creatures . . . they abide friendly and compassionate to all creatures, to all beings.[18]

The great historical example of an attempt to put Buddhism into practice on a nationwide scale occurred during the reign of the Emperor Ashoka, who ruled from about 270 to 232 BC. Ashoka inherited a great empire from his father and grandfather, and during the early years of his reign extended its boundaries even further by conquest. His empire then stretched from the frontier with Persia to the Bay of Bengal. Ashoka had begun his reign by following the traditions of statecraft established by the Brahmins. But after a military victory in Orissa, in which it was said that 100,000 people were killed in battle, even more died for reasons which were incidental to the fighting, and 150,000 people were deported, Ashoka turned to Buddhism.[19] It is probable that there was already sympathy in the family for some of the current criticisms of Brahmin orthodoxy. Ashoka's grandfather, Chandra-gupta, is thought by some to have become an adherent of Jainism at the end of his life, and Ashoka's first wife, Devi, was a lay supporter of the Sangha. The Emperor's conversion to Buddhism appears to have had a great effect upon his own attitudes to kingship and the life of the empire. The Brahmanical tradition which Ashoka had previously followed assumed that kings and emperors would attempt to extend their territory by war, but the Buddhist conception of monarchy taught that a prime duty of the emperor was the cultivation of peace, whether among his own subjects or in relations with neighbouring states.[20]

Evidence of Ashoka's concern for the promulgation of Buddhist ideals has been preserved by the rocks and stone pillars on which he had edicts carved. From the Rock and Pillar Edicts we can obtain a fairly clear view of the nature of the Buddhism which Ashoka had embraced and wished to commend to his people. When all the evidence of Ashoka's understanding of Buddhist dhamma is gathered together it shows that the single most important element in it was non-violence.[21] The Fourth Major Rock Edict declares that *dhamma* involves 'abstention from killing and non-injury to living beings'. The Seventh Pillar Edict says: 'Men have increased their adherence to Dhamma by being persuaded not to injure living beings and not to take life.'[22]

In furtherance of Buddhist principles, the slaughter of animals for food was at first limited and then prohibited in the Emperor's kitchens. The royal fishermen and huntsmen became redundant as their occupations were declared incompatible with Buddhist principles. From being a minority concern of ascetics and *bhikkhus*, the practice of *ahimsa* as it relates to daily food was spreading among the people of India, and the principle of non-injury to living beings was becoming widely accepted. Trevor Ling comments on the Buddhism of Ashoka that,

> for the layman it involved an ethical system whose primary characteristics are non-violence and generosity . . . this code of ethics has remained down to modern times the essence of Buddhism for lay people.[23]

The widespread nature of Ashoka's empire, and the very great influence of Buddhism in India for more than a thousand years, made certain the wholesale dissemination of the ideal of *ahimsa* and the acceptance of the principle of non-violence by many Hindus.

Evidence for the formal adoption of the principle of *ahimsa* by Hindus is to be found in the writing of Patanjali, who lived sometime between 300 and 500 CE, and whose great work, the *Yoga Sutras*, formed the basis for all later teaching of Yoga. Patanjali formulated a system of religious philosophy and practical method which was divided into eight 'limbs', or sections. Together the eight constitute a pathway to the heights of meditation, and include such things as concentration and contemplation. But the first two limbs are concerned with behaviour and attitudes. The first limb is called *yama*, a word which means self-restraint, and is concerned with five vows similar to the basic moral precepts of Jainism and Buddhism. The first of the five is *ahimsa*, understood as abstention from injury to living things together with gentleness towards all. The other four vows are truthfulness, chastity, and refraining from stealing and covetousness.[24]

The eight limbs of Patanjali's Yoga are intended to provide a comprehensive system of behaviour, attitudes, posture and exercises, breathing, and techniques of meditation, but they are also conceived as eight steps leading progressively along a route to spiritual perfection. And the foundation of the first step is *ahimsa*. The advocate of a genuine Indian Yoga would be justified in claiming that the practice of non-violence is a necessary prerequisite of the system.

By the time of Patanjali the ethical basis accepted by Buddhists and Jainas had also been incorporated into a Hindu system. In this, and especially in the emphasis upon *ahimsa*, there was a notable development from the early Hinduism of the Vedas, which had not been at all pacific. The greatest god of the Aryans had been the mighty Indra, who was the god of war and the destroyer of fortified cities. The Aryans, and many later groups who entered India and mixed to form her people, came as military conquerors. But other ideas than those of aggression and conquest had been at work. Varied and conflicting views existed in India, and much evidence of these is to be found in the period between 800 and 300 BC, the time of the composition of the major Upanishads and of the rise of Buddhism and Jainism.

The period of the Upanishads was a time of challenge to the prevailing Brahmanism. But one tradition that persisted from the earliest Vedic times through the Upanishadic period and down to the present day was the practice of caste. The first scriptural reference to a class division in Indian society is found in the *Rig Veda*, where a creation myth tells of the dismembering of a primaeval man to form human society.[25] From the head came the Brahmins, the priests and intellectuals. From his arms was formed the warrior caste, who were called Kshatriya. From his thighs were hewn the Vaishyas, who constituted the merchant class; and from his feet came the Shudra, the labouring people. It is likely that this early division of Indian society reflected the experience of a conquering people imposing themselves upon the conquered and drawing clear lines of demarcation. The light-skinned warlike Aryans had a great contempt for the civilized people of the Indus Valley whom they had conquered. The division referred to in the *Rig Veda* was one way of limiting integration between the two groups and ensuring that the most important functions were reserved to the conquering people. That racial and colour prejudice played its part in the formation of this class structure is suggested by the fact that the word used to describe it is *varna*, a Sanskrit word with the primary meaning of colour.

In the course of time, the simple division of society into four main classes was either elaborated or merged into the caste system, with its thousands of caste and sub-caste groups. But the influence of the four classes can still be seen. The Brahmins remained until modern times clearly the highest caste, with the prerogatives of priestly functions and intellectual leadership. The second group, the Kshatriya, also remain a recognizable grouping of those who inherited the roles of warriors and local princes.

Caste has often been a matter of occupation, an early form of division of labour which over the centuries ossified into a rigid system. Caste determined with whom a Hindu would eat and mix socially, whom he could marry, and what kind of work he could undertake. One of the consequences of the system was that war-like activities were seen to be especially the privilege and duty of members of the warrior castes. Types of work were not inter-changeable. Just as it was the merchant's task to trade and the washerman's task to wash the villagers' clothes, so it was the warrior's task to fight when necessity arose. So at least one his-torian of India regards caste attitude as a major factor in the defeat of Hindus by Muslim invaders from 1000 CE onwards.[26] Large sections of the population were content to regard fighting as someone else's job. Here, perhaps, is one reason for the grow-ing attraction of the idea of *ahimsa* in India: it was possible, as it was not in Europe, for considerable sections of the population to avoid participation in directly warlike activities. It is, however, a kind of irony that two of the greatest advocates of *ahimsa*, Gau-tama the Buddha and Ashoka, came from families of the warrior class.

Alongside the division of tasks among the people at large ran the system which divided a man's life into periods of worldly and other-worldly activities. The ideal which was held before high caste Hindus, as we have seen, suggested a division of his life into four stages. As a boy he should be attached to a guru, who would teach him the scriptures and elements of spiritual wisdom. As a young man he should marry and raise a family, living in the world and accepting the compromises to the ideals of chastity and *ahimsa* that this involves. When the family was old enough to support itself, and the mother, the father should take himself off to the forest to live a life of quiet contemplation with a number of like-minded men. And finally he should adopt the life-style of the *sannyasi*, renouncing all the normal comforts of life in order to prepare most effectively for death and rebirth. The four stages represented an ideal, and only a small proportion of Hindus would ever have followed through all four. But it did suggest that the quest for the higher reaches of spiritual life, with a serious and absolute pursuit of chastity, non-violence, truthfulness, and not stealing or coveting, was something to be undertaken outside the framework of ordinary everyday life. The ethical values them-selves did not have to accord with the realities of daily life. In the life of the householder, it was accepted, compromises would have to be made.

So Hindu scriptures came to be applied to a complex social situation, in which a person's caste largely determined the application that would be given to ideas expounded in the Upanishads and the Epics. The ethical ideas of Hinduism were also subject to variations caused by the stage of life or the degree of withdrawal from daily life of any particular individual.

No consistent view about *ahimsa* and its application to the life of society is to be found in Hindu scriptures. The Vedas, as we have seen, incorporate the ideals of a warlike people. In the Upanishads a more reflexive and philosophical attitude is found. The Upanishads are an important source for the monistic philosophy of *advaita*, which sees divinity in all things and all things as part of the divine *brahman*, and so tends to encourage an attitude of reverence for life. Human and animal life is to be cared for partly because everything is part of a whole; in injuring another we injure ourselves. As the modern Hindu writer Nikhilananda puts it: 'In the doctrine of non-dualism is found the real explanation of the great commandment to love one's neighbour as oneself; for one's neighbour is oneself.'[27]

The Epics, which are not regarded as part of revealed scripture but which have immense importance as transmitters of Hindu teaching and values to the mass of Indian people, take an ambivalent attitude towards violence. The Epics are full of stirring stories of heroic exploits by kings and gods, and they include tales of intrigue and violence and warfare. The most well known and best loved of the Epics is the *Bhagavad Gita*, which is part of the great poem, the *Mahabharata*. The *Bhagavad Gita* has been used in modern times as a text for non-violence, and yet on a straightforward reading seems a curious choice for such use. The story which forms the background of the Gita is of a great battle at Kurukshetra, in northern India, between two related groups, the Kauravas and the Pandavas. The story may have some historical basis in the dim past in rivalries between and within the small kingdoms of India. But the hero of the *Gita* is none other than the god Krishna, the avatara or incarnation of Lord Vishnu. He appears in the guise of the chariot driver of Arjuna, one of the Pandava brothers. Arjuna is tormented by doubts. He surveys the armies drawn up for battle and is overcome by remorse at the sight of his kinsmen on the other side. How can he take part in such a battle? The *Gita* purports to be the answer of Lord Krishna to this quandary.

The answer is at several levels. Arjuna is a Kshatriya, and so it is his duty to fight. Duty, or *dharma*, is heavily emphasized in the *Gita*, and it is closely related to the obligations of caste. 'Better to perform your own *dharma* badly than another's *dharma* well. Better to find death in one's own *dharma*, for the *dharma* of another has only fear for you.'[28] The Kshatriya must fight, for it is his duty. This apparently simple resolution of moral conflict has considerable appeal still in an India in which duty relates to caste. I recall hearing a well-known speaker on religious topics brush aside questions about the rightness of participation in one of the border wars between India and Pakstan in the 1960s by saying of Indian Air Force pilots, 'They are modern day Kshatriyas. It is their duty to fight.' And that was the end of the discussion!

The *Gita* also answers Arjuna's dilemma by reference to Indian philosophy. What is killed in battle is only the body of the opponent; his soul will go on to another birth. The person who slays him has only hastened the process, and perhaps even done him a favour.

These may appear to be unlikely grounds on which to base a programme of non-violent resistance. Yet the *Gita* was one of Gandhiji's favourite texts.

Mahatma Gandhi solved the problem of the *Gita* by allegorizing it. For him the battlefield of Kurukshetra was a spiritual battlefield, on which every person contends for good or evil. The story was regarded simply as a convenient way of reciting religious truth. But the essential thing about the *Gita* for Gandhiji was the idea of *nishkama karma*. The *Gita* has much to say about the importance of *karma*, or action. To do one's work rightly is seen to be very important. And best of all is to do one's duty without any thought of praise or blame, in complete detachment. Do what *dharma* dictates whatever the consequences may be, without any desire for reward or any fear of suffering. In the *Gita* the doctrine of *nishkama karma* is recommended to Arjuna, who must do his duty as a warrior whatever the consequences may be. In Gandhi's teaching this was a hallowed example of the spirit of non-violent resistance, of doing what was right because it was right in the confidence that truth and righteousness must then prevail. No threat of *lathi* charge or imprisonment should be allowed to deflect the person of non-violence from the path of right and duty. Detached from fear of punishment and the longing for praise alike, the non-violent resister would strive for the goal of independence in a positive spirit of love, but with a fearful tenacity.

Detachment and renunciation have played a large part in the history of Hinduism since the tumultuous centuries between 800 and 300 BC. In modern times they became corner-stones of a reinterpretation of the doctrine of *ahimsa*.

4

An Apostle of Non-Violence

Mohandas Karamchand Gandhi was born in Gujarat on 2 October 1869. His family was highly respectable and orthodox, with a deep attachment to Hindu religion and a high regard for patterns of social acceptance which are so important a part of practical Hinduism.

The Gandhis belonged to the Bania caste, which may be broadly located within the third general grouping of Hindu *varna*, the Vaishya or merchant group.[1] The Banias were originally grocers, but Gandhi's recent family had achieved distinction in government. His grandfather, father, and uncle had all served as Prime Ministers in the Kathiawad Princely States. Kaba Gandhi, the father of Mohandas, was Prime Minister in Rajkot and then in Vankaner.

The Hindu caste system is complex and, as with much Indian life, full of paradoxes. The Banias are not especially high caste, and certainly nowhere near to the exclusive status of, say, the Kashmiri Brahmin group to which Jawarhalal Nehru belonged. But the Banias do have a reputation for strict orthodoxy, the observance of vegetarianism, and other high-caste practices.[2] Such behaviour not infrequently reflects a desire on the part of groups in the middle of the caste hierarchy to improve their status; hence the paradox of middle-caste groups sometimes being more orthodox in their observance of high-caste practices than the high castes themselves.

Such was the social background of the Gandhis. The first three wives of Kaba Gandhi died, and it was his fourth wife, Putlibai, who was the mother of Mohandas. Gandhiji described his mother as a deeply religious woman, and his abiding memory of her was of a saintly character.[3] She was a daily visitor to the local Vaishnava temple, engaged in frequent fasts, and often took solemn vows to fast for particular periods.

Gandhi's childhood, then, was spent in an atmosphere of probity, public service, great emphasis upon the importance of caste practice, especially in relation to vegetarianism, and simple Hindu devotion. The influence of this home background is evident in the whole later life of Mohandas Gandhi.

One other factor in Gandhiji's background is of particular relevance to his later history. The India in which he was born was, of course, under British dominance. The gradual growth of British military and political power in India under the East India Company had given way to the direct government of India by the Crown in 1858 – one of the consequences of the turbulent months between May 1857 and June 1858 referred to by British historians as 'The Indian Mutiny' and by Indian historians as 'The Indian Revolt'. Not until Gandhi was eight years old, however, was Queen Victoria proclaimed Empress of India, in 1876. But even then direct British rule was not established over the whole of India. There were many ostensibly independent states, ruled by their own princes. British Residents were often stationed in the capitals of princely states to 'advise' the local ruler and to ensure that British interests in such matters as defence and trade were carefully guarded. But the princely states did have a measure of independence, and they preserved areas of India from undue influence of British culture and from the presence of very large numbers of foreigners. Gujarat was an area of India that did not come under direct British rule and remained relatively free of foreign influence.

The area was also one which had been influenced by Jainism, and there was close contact between the Gandhi family and Jaina monks, some of whom frequently visited Gandhi's father in Rajkot.[4] Jain influence gave added importance to ascetic practices among the Hindus, including strict vegetarianism, the avoidance of alcohol, and the practice of *ahimsa*.[5] The strength of local feeling and the particular situation of Gujarat towards the end of the nineteenth century added to family influence in laying the foundations of Mohandas Gandhi's character and attitudes.

The more general background of Indian history during Gandhiji's early childhood also reflected some of the political and economic issues which sharpened the conflict of interest between Indians aspiring to a greater say in the control of their own country and Englishmen determined to maintain the political advantages which the control of India brought. A threat to British interests much feared in the late nineteenth century was the southwards advance of Russia towards Afghanistan and the north-western borders of India.[6] In 1867 Russia established her new province of Turkestan, with its headquarters at Tashkent, and the following year took Samarqand. Russia's supposed designs upon India caused much consternation in Britain and British India, and provided the British justification for the launching of the Second Afghan War in 1878.

For the British, India was not simply a possession valued for its economic benefits and the opportunities it presented for practising the art of bearing the white man's burden; it was also a vital part of the chain of British political dominance forged around much of the world in the nineteenth century. From a Victorian perspective it appeared that British interests necessitated the control of India.

On the other hand, the early years of Mohandas Gandhi's life were marked by a new phase in the reform movements of India. Wearied by centuries of Muslim dominance, Hindu culture and religion were at a low ebb in the early nineteenth century, when it had to face the new and menacing threats posed by European culture, Western scientific and technological expertise, the use of the English language for education in India, and the activities of Christian missionaries. The initial response of Hindu intellectuals was to reform Hinduism in the light of Western criticism. But around 1870 a change of mood can be discerned in the reform movements. Reformers began to assert to Europeans and to their own countrymen the abiding values of Hindu religion and culture, and to affirm their equality with, or even superiority to, Western forms of religious belief, moral values and cultural mores. This process of renewal was a vital part of the growth of self-confidence and national pride which underlay the development of Indian nationalism at the end of the nineteenth century. Religious and cultural renewal in India was closely linked with the rise of nationalist feelings, and provided an essential element in a feeling of national self-confidence which was to lead to direct political action. In 1885, when Gandhi was sixteen, the first meeting of the Indian National Congress was held. Although at first the aims of the Congress were very modest, the formation of that organization marked the beginnings of a political movement towards Indian independence.

Mohandas spent his first seven years in Porbandar, and then moved with the family to Rajkot. He appears to have been a child of great moral earnestness but of only modest ability in other directions. His schooling was not marked by any notes of distinction, and he later said of himself that, 'I could only have been a mediocre student.'[7] However, he did develop a love of Hindu devotional literature, especially the Hindi version of the Ramayana by Tulsidas.[8]

A crucial event in Gandhi's early years was his marriage at the age of only thirteen to Kasturbai. It was customary among Hindu families at the time for the marriage of children to be arranged when they were very young, and for marriages to be consummated as soon as the children reached puberty. Gandhi's marriage to Kasturbai was part of an arrangement which included the marriage of a brother, two or three years older, and a cousin who was one year older. In later life Gandhi greatly regretted this early marriage not only because it seemed utterly inappropriate for two young children – 'I can see no moral argument in support of such a preposterously early marriage'[9] – but also because of the feelings of guilt and shame towards sexual activity which later became marked features of the Mahatma's ascetic life-style. He was particularly guilt-ridden because of the circumstances of his father's death, when Gandhi was sixteen. Filial devotion is an important element of Hindu society, and Gandhi was glad of the opportunity to express his affection for his father by sitting by Kaba Gandhi's bed during his last illness and massaging him to give him some relief from pain. On the night his father died Gandhi had been by his side as usual, and had then retired to his wife's bed for the night. Five or six minutes later a servant came to Gandhi's room to tell him that his father had died. Gandhi was assailed then and ever afterwards by guilt. He had, he felt, deserted his father at the moment of his greatest need, and this experience appears to have saddled the young Gandhi with an enormous load of guilt which he associated especially with sex.

> I saw that, if animal passion had not blinded me, I should have been spared the torture of separation from my father during his last moments . . . It is a blot I have never been able to efface or forget.[10]

His remorse was increased by the fact that his wife was also pregnant at the time, and contemporary tradition, accepted entirely by Gandhi, suggested that sexual activity at such a time was dangerous.

> Every night whilst my hands were busy massaging my father's legs, my mind was hovering about the bedroom, and that too

at a time when religion, medical science and common sense alike forbade sexual intercourse.[11]

It seemed to Gandhi that the justice of his guilt was confirmed when the baby born to his wife died within three or four days. 'Nothing else could be expected,' Gandhi wrote illogically but with absolute conviction.

This early experience of Gandhi, together with local Hindu and Jaina ascetic traditions which coloured his childhood, confirmed in him a curious and apparently ambivalent attitude towards sexual activity which was important in his later life. In common with many Hindus – although, be it noted, not all, for the Tantric tradition of pursuing divine union through physical union is also part of Hinduism – Gandhi regarded *brahmacharya*, or celibacy, as a necessary prerequisite of spiritual growth. He took a 'vow' of *brahmacharya* in 1905, after nearly twenty-four years of marriage, apparently after much strugggling with his natural desires, and he claimed never to have had sexual relationships with his wife after that time. This, he thought, was an important contributory factor to spiritual advance and to the practice of non-violence. He taught that the only legitimate function of sexual activity was the procreation of children, and seriously advocated the absurdly unrealistic measure of restraint from sex as the answer to India's population problem.

But celibacy does not appear to have come easily to Gandhi. His struggles with the claims of sex produced in his later life some bizarre incidents which have been investigated by Ved Mehta in his fine biography of Gandhi.[12] Mehta took much trouble during the writing of his book to tour India to meet and talk to as many of Gandhi's followers as he could. He interviewed a number of people, now mostly elderly, who were young disciples of the Mahatma during the independence struggle. And he records comments about the curious 'experiments with *brahmacharya*' conducted by Gandhi. This included the practice of Gandhi, in his sixties and seventies, sleeping with young women. He took pride in the claim that to spend the night with a young naked woman by his side did not awaken in him any sexual desires. Mehta wrote:

> In Noakhali, Gandhi publicly disclosed the fact that he had been taking naked girls to bed with him for years, but had tried to keep the practice secret in order to avoid public controversy.[13]

Many among Gandhi's followers, especially the men, were perturbed by this practice and by the scandal it might create. But the

Mahatma refused to make any concession to their feelings. According to Mehta's interviews, the girls who were involved in the experiments, and who also often occupied the roles of attendants, nurses, and secretaries to Gandhiji, were happy to perform these services for him and sometimes jealously possessive of his reliance upon them.[14]

Was all this simply repressed sexuality and guilt, together with the results of a puritanical Hindu upbringing? Gandhi himself was quite open about the personal details of his life – indeed, so public was most of his life that all he did was common knowledge to a large number of people. For him, *brahmacharya* was an essential part of spiritual progress and the practice of non-violence. But there can be little doubt that hidden from his own conscious mind were repressed desires which indicated how unnatural were parts of his life, and how little suited to serve as a model for others. Gandhi had sensed something of the important links between deep religious feeling and sexuality, but it seems most unlikely that he interpreted them correctly.

The death of his father was a traumatic event for Gandhi, but life went on and he had to face the demands placed upon him by his family and their expectations. In 1887 he became a student at Samaldas College, in Bhavnagar. It is unlikely that the standards of such a college would have been high at that time, but apparently they were too high for Mohandas Gandhi. After one term he dropped out of college. There appears to have been no external pressure on him to do so, and it is astonishing that somebody who was later to show such powers of mind and heart should have failed a modest college course.[15] But such was the case. The family were perturbed about the effects this would have upon his future career, and they conferred together as to what could be done for him. A family friend, Mavji Dave, suggested that the boy should be sent to England to study law. To become a lawyer in India would have been a lengthy and difficult business, for he would first have had to have completed a BA degree course and then have studied law. But in England the situation was different. Astonishing as it may seem by comparison with today's high standards, it was then a comparatively easy matter, given the right connections and the funds, to qualify as a barrister in England. Within two or three years, at the expense of only very modest gifts and effort, it was possible to become a barrister – then to practise at the bar was no doubt much more difficult, but for a foreign student that did not matter. Gandhi was delighted with the suggestion.

Nothing could have been more welcome to me. I was fighting shy of difficult studies. So I jumped at the proposal and said that the sooner I was sent the better.[16]

But the suggestion was not without its difficulties. Until well into the twentieth century, high caste Hindus frowned upon the practice of caste members 'crossing the black waters' by going to foreign countries where they would be outside the control and supervision of their own social group, and where the observance of important caste practices relating to social mixing and diet might be impossible. Gandhi's mother was worried about the implications of her son going so far away from home to live on his own in a strange country, and she was only persuaded to assent when Gandhi took his vow to abstain from wine, women and meat. Other members of the caste were not so easily satisfied. No Modh Bania had previously been to England. A special meeting of members of the community was called, and Gandhi summoned to appear before it. He was told that in the opinion of the community it would be impossible to observe caste practices in England, and ordered not to go.[17] By this time, however, Gandhi had made up his mind and was not to be deterred from what he regarded as a great adventure and an unrivalled opportunity. The community declared him an outcaste, and threatened any caste member who helped him on his way with a fine. For Gandhi the promised benefits of his visit to England were more important than the censure of his community. His immediate family had given their approval, and he saw the plan as one that would be helpful to them in the long run by enabling him to earn a good living to the benefit of the whole family. And clearly by this time the adventure had captured his imagination. He would go.

On 4 September 1888 Gandhi sailed from Bombay. He found himself at once in a strange environment, and it was to take him many months to come to terms with European conventions. His first problem on board ship was simply that of communicating with people in English. (Was his failure at Samaldas College, perhaps, the result of the problem experienced by generations of Indian students entering higher education and having to switch from their native language to English?) The food was strange to him, and since he was quite determined to abide by his vow not to touch meat, additional problems arose at every meal. Gandhi's strict adherence to vegetarianism during that voyage and throughout his stay in England says much for his strength of character. The temptations to accept the customs of the people among whom he found himself must have been very strong, especially when he was told repeatedly by people with kindly intentions that it was quite impossible to live in the cold climate of England without recourse to meat and alcohol. When he became settled in England and began to make a few friends, he was greatly helped by the Vegetarian Society, of which he became an enthusiastic member and eventually a member of the Society's Executive Committee.[18]

Gandhi's studies in England were successful, but as his autobiography shows, they were not regarded by him as the most important element of his English experience. During his first year in England, anxious to improve his English and his command of language, Gandhi took the London Matriculation examination (then the basic qualification for entry to a degree course). It was necessary to take Latin and a modern European language among the five subjects that made up the examination, and although Gandhi passed only at his second attempt, it is a mark of his industry at this time that he gained sufficient knowledge of Latin and French to enable him to matriculate. His examinations for the bar he does not seem to have regarded as difficult, although he suggested that the obligation he felt to read all the stipulated text-books involved him in more labour than was usual for most of the students. His reading stood him in good stead, however, and he passed the examinations on 10 June 1891, enrolled in the High Court on the following day, and on 12 June sailed for home.

Whilst in England, however, Gandhi had extended his knowledge in areas other than law. At the end of his second year in the country he met two brothers who were both Theosophists.[19] They encouraged him to read the *Bhagavad Gita* with them. In spite of his childhood acquaintance with parts of the great Epics of India, Gandhi had not previously read the *Gita*, and felt a little ashamed that he had not read it in either Gujarati or Sanskrit and had to come to it first in English. They read the *Gita* together in Sir Edwin Arnold's translation, Gandhi supplementing their reading with comments based upon his own 'meagre' understanding of Sanskrit.[20] The book made an enormous impression on him, and ever afterwards it provided him with a basic religious text from which to substantiate his views on religion and life. He wrote of that first reading:

> The book struck me as one of priceless worth. The impression has ever since been growing on me with the result that I regard it today as the book par excellence for the knowledge of Truth.[21]

What Gandhi found in the *Gita* was justification for the view that the essence of religion – not just Hinduism, but all religion – has to do with renunciation. The *Gita* speaks in places of the need to perform the actions and duties which religion and society prescribe in a spirit of indifference, without thought of reward or fear of unpleasant consequences. This particular aspect of the *Gita*'s teaching fitted well with the ideas Gandhi was to develop later of the principle of non-violence, and he was to regard the *Bhagavad Gita* as the most important religious text for the non-violent activist.

In the light of modern scholarship on the *Gita* (or, indeed, of a straightforward reading of the text) this appears to be a curious doctrine to have culled from this source. The story of the *Gita* is of Arjuna the warrior being told by Lord Krishna to overcome his aversion to slaughtering his kinsmen in battle and to perform the duty of his caste. As a Kshatriya, Arjuna's duty was to fight. Better to do the duty of one's caste badly than to commit the cardinal sin of adopting the role of another caste or ignoring caste altogether.[22] The supposition of a number of modern scholars that the *Gita* was in part a text against the Buddhists, who broke caste, would appear to be plausible.[23]

Comfort is offered to Arjuna by setting the stern command to do this duty against a background of Samkhya philosophy. The soul cannot be killed: only the body, transient and therefore in some sense illusory, is destroyed.[24] What harm, then, is done? Reinforcing this argument is the doctrine of *nishkama karma*, which stresses the virtue of doing one's own duty without fear of the consequences.[25] The only pure action is that which is performed without regard for praise or blame, status or reward, loss or suffering.

How can the *Bhagavad Gita* be an authority for the man or woman of non-violence?

Gandhiji solved the problem by allegorizing the *Gita*.[26] The battlefield of the story, he suggested, is really the human soul, on which is fought the continuing battle between good and evil. It was a device which satisfied Gandhi who, after all, tended to draw from scriptures and other inspirational writing whatever appealed to him. But it is doubtful whether in this way he successfully grounded *satyagraha* in the mainstream of Hindu tradition, and this he himself seems to have understood.

I have admitted in my introduction to the Gita known as An-asakti Yoga that it is not a treatise on non-violence nor was it written to condemn war. Hinduism as it is practised today, or has ever been known to have ever been practised, has certainly not condemned war as I do. What, however, I have done is to put a new but natural and logical interpretation upon the whole teaching of the Gita and the spirit of Hinduism. Hinduism, not to speak of other religions, is ever evolving. . . . I have endeavoured, in the light of prayerful study of the other faiths of the world and, what is more, in the light of my own experience in trying to live Hinduism as interpreted in the Gita, to give an extended but in no way strained meaning to Hinduism.[27]

Gandhi's fulsome praise for the *Gita* was to be expressed years later in a small book which he wrote, called *Gita – My Mother*, in which he made clear that the *Gita* had been a constant source of inspiration and guidance to him. But it was certainly the *Gita*'s teaching on *karma yoga*, and the idea that one's duty was to be performed regardless of praise or blame, reward or punishment, that Gandhi extracted from the *Gita* and made a cornerstone of the theory and practice of non-violent resistance.

It was also whilst he was in England that Gandhi undertook his first reading of the Bible. He was introduced to the Christian scriptures by a friend he met in a Manchester vegetarian boarding house. The Christian acquaintance appears to have omitted any guidance on how the Bible was to be read. Gandhi started at the beginning, found the early books of the Old Testament unrewarding reading, and solemnly confessed a lack of enthusiasm for the Book of Numbers. The New Testament, however, evoked a more enthusiastic response:

But the New Testament produced a different impression, especially the Sermon on the Mount, which went straight to my heart. I compared it with the Gita. The verses, 'But I say unto you, that ye resist not evil: but whosoever shall smite thee on thy right cheek, turn to him the other also. And if any man take away thy coat let him have thy cloak too' delighted me beyond measure. . . My young mind tried to unify the teaching of the Gita, The Light of Asia, and the Sermon on the Mount. That renunciation was the highest form of religion appealed to me greatly.[28]

Gandhi's method with religious material is apparent here. His reading on the whole was random. He selected passages that appealed to him personally, and then he gave an interpretation which was not conditioned by dreary questions of background, context, language, or any other of the considerations which must be weighed by the scholar.

That the Sermon on the Mount is concerned primarily with renunciation is far from likely. A more acceptable interpretation of Matthew 5–7 would regard this section as a collection of sayings which provide vivid illustrations of the nature of the love exhibited by a God of grace and, therefore, to be emulated by those who worship him.[29]

It is also interesting to note that, although Gandhi allegorized the *Gita*, he applied a literal interpretation to the Sermon on the Mount.

When Gandhi returned to India in the summer of 1891, he found that the problems of equipping himself to earn a living and pursue a satisfactory career had not been solved entirely by his studies in England. He had qualified as a barrister; but, of course, he had never practised law. In England it was more difficult to become established as a practising barrister than it was simply to qualify as one. It was even more difficult to establish oneself in India, where there were different laws to be considered and different practices connected with court procedures and the feeding of cases to lawyers. Gandhi found that he knew next to nothing about the business of making a living as a lawyer in India, in spite of his impressive English qualification. He went to Bombay for a while, hoping to have some success in the courts there, but returned to Rajkot a failure. There, he began to earn a modest living by drafting applications and memorials for clients rather than by arguing in court. And then came an offer which was to change the course of his life.

There was at the time a considerable number of Indians living in South Africa. Initially Tamils and Gujaratis had been taken to South Africa as indentured labour. Some had settled there when their indentures were finished. And merchants, many of them Gujaratis, had followed the labourers to ply their own trade. A considerable Indian community had been established in South Africa, especially in the area around Durban.

A Meman, or Muslim, firm from Porbandar was engaged in business in Durban, and found itself involved in a court case for a claim of some £40,000. Through their contacts in Gujarat they suggested that Gandhi should go to South Africa to work for a period on their behalf 'so that he could instruct our counsel better than ourselves'. He was expected to be away for not more than a year, and his payment was to be his first-class return fare, together with his living expenses and payment of £105.[30]

In April 1893 Gandhi sailed to South Africa. He then had no idea that apart from brief visits back to India South Africa was to remain his home until 1914. And it was to be in fighting for the rights of Indian residents suffering from racially discriminatory laws that Gandhi was to develop his ideas and techniques of non-violent resistance.

The racial intolerance of South Africa came as a surprise to Gandhi. He had lived in England, and there had found that racial prejudice counted for little. In the later years of the nineteenth century, class was much more important than race in marking the social divisions in Britain, and well-educated Indians like Gandhi found themselves widely accepted. He had noticed on his return to India that relationships with Englishmen, even those he had met in England, were on a different basis and that race and colonialism had much in common. But racialism in South Africa was a new experience for him.

When he had been only seven or eight days in South Africa, Gandhi had to make a journey from Durban to Pretoria. Dressed as an English barrister would dress, and with his own self-image as a member of an elite profession, Gandhi naturally took a first-class ticket, and began the journey with a compartment to himself. When the train reached Maritzburg, however, a white passenger came to occupy a seat in the compartment and took exception to Gandhi's presence there. The white man called railway officials, who in turn fetched a policeman. Gandhi refused to do as he was asked, and transfer to the 'van compartment', and so he was turned off the train to spend an uncomfortable night on the station at Maritzburg. For the first time he had realized that the price of one's ticket or the status of one's profession could be much less important than the colour of one's skin in determining social acceptance.

On another occasion Gandhi was travelling by coach and horses from Charlestown to Johannesburg and was required to sit outside, beside the driver, whilst the 'leader' of the coach team sat inside in Gandhi's place. When the leader wanted a smoke, he asked Gandhi to make room for him by the driver by sitting on the footboard. When Gandhi refused, 'the man came down upon me and began heavily to box my ears'.[31] Although Gandhi complained to the coach company about his treatment, he refused to take any action against the man who had assaulted him. At the end of that particular journey the contemporary racial attitudes in South Africa were confirmed when Gandhi was refused a room at the Grand National Hotel in Johannesburg.[32]

During his first year in South Africa Gandhi was already concerned about the legal position of Indians in Natal and the Transvaal. In The Transvaal, for instance, Indians were required to pay a poll tax of £3 in order to enter the territory. They could not own land, except under restrictive conditions in certain townships; they were not permitted to walk on public footpaths; they were not allowed out of doors after 9.00 p.m.; and they had no vote.

Resentment among white South Africans was growing over the fact that many Indians who had arrived in the country as indentured labour were staying on when their indentures were completed. In addition, of course, the presence of indentured labourers brought the Indian traders who began by trading with the Indian community but who, the whites feared, would end by becoming more successful than their white counterparts. There was particular resentment among the poorer and less successful white shopkeepers over what they regarded as unfair competition. Colonial ambitions which had taken the Europeans to South Africa were reinforced by assumptions about white racial superiority, and Indians were regarded as inferior and uncouth people who would lower expectations and standards of life in the country if once they become a numerically significant part of the population. The fact that the first Indian settlers had been indentured labourers had created the impression that most Indians were at the educational and cultural level of the labourer. The word 'coolie' was used indiscriminately of all Indians; even Gandhi was referred to as a 'coolie barrister', apparently without any sense of incongruity.

The case for which Gandhi had gone to South Africa ended, and he prepared to leave for home. At a farewell party given in his honour, Gandhi happened to glance through some newspapers and noticed reports of a Bill then passing through the Natal Legislative Assembly which proposed to deprive Indians of their right to elect members to the Assembly. At the last moment Gandhi changed his plans and agreed with the leaders of the Indian community to stay in South Africa to attempt to lead a movement amongst the Indians against the disabilities under which they laboured. Gandhi would not accept payment for the work he proposed to undertake, although he made it clear that considerable funds would have to be raised in order to carry on a successful campaign. For his own keep he planned to engage in legal work on his own account, and he was eventually to build a prosperous practice in South Africa. But his motive for staying in the country, and his chief concern for the next twenty years, was to be 'public work'.

In addition to material connected with political and legal work, however, Gandhi continued to read many books on moral and religious themes during his early years in South Africa. Before leaving India he had made the acquaintance of a Jaina merchant, Rajchandra Ravjibhai Mehta, or Raychandbhai, who made a great impression on Gandhi. The two corresponded when Gandhi was in Pretoria, and the Jaina ethic of Raychandbhai greatly impressed Gandhi.[33]

His interest in religion was also expressed by conversations he had with a pious Muslim member of the firm of merchants for whom he had gone to South Africa. 'Contact with him,' he said, 'gave me a fair amount of practical knowledge of Islam.'[34]

Gandhi maintained contact with a number of evangelical Christians, attended some Christian services, and seems to have tried his best to understand their position. They were Christians who placed particular stress on the doctrine of the atonement which, not surprisingly, remained something of an enigma to Gandhi.[35] He had also retained links with friends made in London, and when in Natal he acted as the South African agent of 'The Esoteric Christian Union' and the London Vegetarian Society.

A Christian who did make a great impression upon Gandhi was Leo Tolstoy. Gandhi had been attracted by some of the ethical teaching of Christianity, but had been surprised and offended by the failure of Christians to apply such teaching.[36] In Tolstoy he discovered a Christian who was critical of Christian institutions but who was deeply concerned about the application of Christian ideals to social situations. Tolstoy's somewhat unorthodox approach – vigorous criticism of the church as it then was in Russia, a touch of political anarchy, and a strong emphasis upon the absolute demands of Christian love – strongly appealed to Gandhi.

> Tolstoy's *The Kingdom of God is Within You* overwhelmed me. It left an abiding impression on me. Before the independent thinking, profound morality, and the truthfulness of the book, all the books given me by Mr Coates seemed to pale into insignificance.[37]

Later, he made what he described as an 'intensive study' of Tolstoy's books, and as a result said that 'I began to realize more and more the infinite possibilities of universal love.'[38]

Gandhi's reading in South Africa ranged widely, and included Dr Parker's *Commentary*, J. R. Pearson's *Remarkable Providence and Proofs of Divine Revelation*, and Butler's *Analogy*.[39]

During the same period he also read more about Hinduism, studying an English translation of the Upanishads and Max Müller's *India – What Can It Teach Us?* This enhanced his regard for Hinduism. He wrote:

> Thus I gained more knowledge of the different religions. The study stimulated my self-introspection and fostered in me the habit of putting into practice whatever appealed to me in my studies.[40]

So by the end of his first period in South Africa, up to 1896, Gandhi had been influenced in his religious thinking by several different sources – his own Vaishnavite background in Gujarat, his reading of some Hindu texts, the Bible and especially the Sermon on the Mount, and the writings of Tolstoy. Of these, Tolstoy appears to have been the strongest single influence during Gandhiji's first stay in South Africa.

5

Non-Violence in South Africa

Political events determined the course of Gandhi's work in South Africa. The bill denying Indians a franchise in the Natal Legislative Assembly was about to go to its second reading when Gandhi took his decision to remain in South Africa and campaign for the rights of Indians. He recognized that it was too late to prevent the bill being passed, but nevertheless he organized a petition to be presented to the assembly. Once the bill had been passed Gandhi began the organization of a much larger petition – it collected 10,000 signatures – to be presented to Lord Ripon, the Secretary of State for the Colonies.

Gandhi also began to secure his own financial base by beginning work on his own account as a lawyer. He was admitted as a barrister to the Supreme Court in Natal, and even that procedure provided him with an example of the attitudes which were to be met with and responded to by the non-violent resister. Gandhi had retained one item of Indian dress by wearing a turban – a common custom among Indians at the time. Once he had been admitted to the court the judge asked him to remove his turban and abide by the conventions of dress observed by the European lawyers. Gandhi at first was inclined to resist this instruction, just as he had resisted the request to vacate a first-class compartment on the railway when a white passenger entered. But he decided that the issue was not sufficiently serious to warrant a confrontation, and agreed to abide by the judge's request. This, it seemed to him, exemplified the value of compromise.

All my life through, the very insistence on truth has taught me to appreciate the beauty of compromise. I saw in later life that this spirit was an essential part of Satyagraha.[1]

45

In 1894 the first Indian political organization in South Africa was formed with the foundation of the Natal Indian Congress, in part inspired by the existence of the Congress in India, and in part the result of the enthusiasm generated among the Indian community by the petition over the Natal Assembly Bill.[2] Gandhi was the first secretary of the Natal Congress, and in that position he demonstrated his enthusiasm in contacting potential members, in collecting subscriptions, and in writing about the Indian cause. His first two pieces of writing on behalf of the Congress, 'An Appeal to Every Briton in South Africa', and 'Indian Franchise – An Appeal', were widely circulated, and foreshadowed the important part that writing and contact with the press were to play in the later campaigns in which Gandhi took part.

An issue which engaged Gandhi's attention that same year arose out of a proposal of the Natal Government to impose a tax of £25 on any indentured Indian who wished to remain in the country when his indentures expired. The alternatives to paying the tax were either to return to India or to sign fresh indentures. The approval of the government in India was sought for this measure, which reflected the fears of white South Africans over the possible development of a large group of settled and prosperous Indians in the country. The Viceroy in India disagreed with a tax of £25, but agreed to the proposal on condition that the tax be reduced to £3. To Gandhi and other Indian leaders in South Africa this showed clearly how little the Indian Government was prepared to protect the interests of Indians in South Africa. Gandhi organized a public protest over the issue, and later felt that his action had played some part in the Viceroy's decision to insist upon a reduced tax. Nevertheless, the tax was levied not only on the indentured labourer, but also on his wife, any sons over sixteen years and daughters over thirteen years. At a time when the earnings of labourers were between £8 and £9 a year, this was clearly a crippling burden, and one which reflected the determination of the Natal government to prevent the settlement of Indian labourers in their territory.[3]

In 1896 Gandhi returned to India to collect his wife and children. Whilst there he addressed public meetings, had useful contacts with the press, and met many influential people in India, including Lokamanya Tilak, Gokhale, and Surendranath Banerji. Gandhi's reputation was beginning to be known in his own country.

In December Gandhi returned to South Africa to find that his comments about the situations of Indians there had been widely, and not always accurately, reported in the South African press. Public resentment over Gandhi's statements in India had been aroused, and when he arrived at Durban in the company of two shiploads of Indians who had come to settle in South Africa, the resentment boiled over into action. It was assumed by some elements among the South African press that Gandhi had embarked upon a policy of 'swamping' Natal with Indians. The ships were forbidden to land their passengers on the grounds that there had been plague in Bombay when they had left. The passengers had to wait for twenty-three days before they were allowed ashore. But even then, large crowds were waiting for Gandhi, who had to be smuggled ashore secretly. He was later recognized in the street, and set upon by an angry crowd. Bruised and battered, he eventually escaped with the help of the police, and in the long run felt that the experience created a certain amount of public sympathy for him.

During the 1890s Gandhi was already committed to the idea of non-violence, although the term *satyagraha* had not yet been coined. But the influence of his notion of renunciation as the keynote of religion, his understanding of *nishkama karma* in the *Bhagavad Gita*, his reading of the Sermon on the Mount and of Tolstoy, had reinforced the traditions of *ahimsa* he had learned as a child and convinced him that the non-violent approach to situations of conflict expressed an essential element of true religion and morality.

This non-violent approach, however, did not involve a doctrinaire pacifism. A clear example of the difference between non-violence and absolute pacifism was provided by Gandhi's response to the Boer War, which began in 1899. Politically, Gandhi saw himself as involved in an attempt to secure rights due to citizens of the British Empire for the Indians in South Africa. He subscribed to the notional ideal of an Empire citizenship in which all citizens were theoretically equal, and assumed that when inequalities were made sufficiently clear to British authorities they would, in the name of the justice of the Empire, establish equality. This being his position, Gandhi thought it right to support the British cause in war against opponents of the Empire. So he encouraged Indians in South Africa to support the British in the Boer War, and he gave practical expression to that support by organizing an ambulance corps composed of Indian volunteers.[4] Of course, his volunteers were non-combatants, but they did accept military discipline and the wearing of uniform, and there seems little doubt that Gandhi saw them not only as servants of mercy and compassion but also as a visible expression of Indian support for the British in their struggle against the Boers.

With the end of the Boer War Gandhi believed his usefulness in South Africa to be at an end, and he returned to India and took some preliminary steps to establish himself as a barrister in Bombay. He assumed that the proof of loyalty given by the Indian community during the war would have convinced the Europeans of the rightness of equality, and that in future there would be no major problems for Indian settlers. But in this he was wrong. The position of Indians in some areas of South Africa deteriorated after the war. Certainly this happened in the Transvaal, which before the Boer War had been essentially a foreign country to the British. In that situation the British Government had been willing to exert itself to some extent on behalf of Indians who were British subjects; and the majority of whites in the Transvaal were not British subjects. But when as a result of the Boer War the Transvaal was annexed, 'the Imperial Government undertook . . . to administer the country in accordance with the wishes of the people of the country themselves'.[5]

The idea of 'separate development', later so familiar a part of the South African scene, was already being canvassed in the Transvaal in 1901. The Commissioner for Mines, W. Wybergh, suggested that public vehicles should be for Europeans only or Coloured persons only, and that, 'Within the European quarter no Asiatic should be allowed to reside or carry on any business in person and the same should apply to Europeans within the Asiatic quarters.'[6] The Transvaal authorities planned the establishment of fifty-four special locations for Indians, although it was suggested that 'well-educated' Indians might be granted exemption from the need to live in such a location.

Gandhi had promised to return to South Africa if ever he were needed, and in November 1902 the Indian community urged him to do so. As well as general disappointment at the situation, there was felt to be a specific need for Gandhi's presence during a visit to South Africa of Joseph Chamberlain, then Secretary of State for the Colonies. So Gandhi returned, this time establishing himself in the Transvaal rather than Natal, and setting up his lawyer's office in Johannesburg.

In addition to earning himself a living, Gandhi was busy organizing the Indian community and publicizing their cause in South Africa, India, and Britain. In 1904 he began the publication of *Indian Opinion*, a weekly journal which provided a vital means of communication with Indians in South Africa, and which, together with the later publications *Young India* and *Harijan*, has preserved a very full record of Gandhi's thought and action over a period of nearly forty years. *Indian Opinion* was issued at first in Hindi, Gujarati, Tamil and English, but the Hindi and Tamil editions were soon discontinued.[7]

In October 1904 Gandhi read a book which was to have a decisive effect on his life. A Christian friend, Mr Polak, gave Gandhi a copy of Ruskin's *Unto This Last* to read on a train journey between Johannesburg and Durban. Gandhi said of it:

> The book was impossible to lay aside once I had begun it. . .
> I determined to change my life in accordance with the ideals of
> the book.[8]

These ideals he understood to be:

1. That the good of the individual is contained in the good of all.
2. That a lawyer's work has the same value as the barber's, inasmuch as all have the same right of earning their livelihood from their work.
3. That a life of labour, i.e., the life of a tiller of the soil and the handicraftsman, is the life worth living.

The first of these I knew. The second I had dimly realized. The third had never occurred to me.[9]

He later translated Ruskin's book into Gujarati, under the title of *Sarvodaya* (the welfare, or uplift, of all). It had a great influence upon Gandhi's social thought, and upon his attempts to identify with the poor and to abolish untouchability.

One consequence of the reading of Ruskin's book was that Gandhi conceived the idea of founding a settlement where some of his associates and followers could live as a community and attempt to put into practice the ideals of *sarvodaya*. A piece of land was purchased near Phoenix, some fourteen miles from Durban, a community established, and *Indian Opinion* began to be published from Phoenix Farm. Here began the experiments, later continued in the Gandhian ashrams in India, in which people were expected to live together without regard to caste distinctions, and where all were expected to engage in even the most laborious and menial tasks of the community. A virtue was made of simple living, of sharing household tasks, and of as much self-subsistence as possible. Gandhi himself was not able to share fully in the life of Phoenix in the first years because of the need to attend to his office in Johannesburg, and it was not until 1906 that he sent his family to live there. But the experiment was of great importance, and played a significant part in creating the sense of solidarity and loyalty to a common cause which underlay the early developments of the movement of non-violent resistance.

Gandhi's attitude to warfare was tested again in 1906, when the Zulu Rebellion erupted in Natal. Again, a sense of loyalty to the Empire encouraged Gandhi to organize a small corps of stretcher bearers to serve with the British troops. The work lasted for only a few weeks, and Gandhi declared himself glad that he had acted as he did, for his stretcher-bearers, he wrote, had been able to give help to wounded Zulus who otherwise would not have been attended.

Once again, however, loyalty to the British Empire did not seem to result in equality and justice for the Indian community. The Zulu Rebellion was in June and July 1906. In September of that year there was published the Draft Asiatic Ordinance (Transvaal), which was aimed at strictly controlling the movement of Asians into the Transvaal and rendering them subject to strict control whilst there. The Draft Ordinance required that every Indian of eight years or above 'lawfully resident' in the Transvaal should register with the Registrar of Asiatics, and give their finger or thumb impression as proof of identity. Any India failing to register would thereby forfeit the right to reside in the Transvaal. 'Failure to apply would be held to be an offence in law for which the defaulter could be fined, sent to prison or even deported within the discretion of the court.'[10] Certificates of registration would have to be produced before any police officer who required it, and failure to produce the certificate would also be an offence, punishable by fine or imprisonment.

The publication of the Draft Ordinance shocked and surprised Gandhi and the Indian community; but it was consistent with the policy of the Transvaal Government towards Indians. In August 1905 Lord Selbourne, the High Commissioner, argued strongly in a despatch to the foreign office for a ban on future Indian immigration. He wanted English settlers for the Transvaal, for they would surely resist the Boers in any future confrontation. But in his capacity as a trader, he felt, 'the white British subject is hopelessly beaten out of the field by the Asiatic'.[11]

Nevertheless, Gandhi was amazed by the harshness of the proposals. 'I have never known legislation of this nature being directed against free men in any part of the world.'[12] A meeting of Indians was held on 11 September to protest at the measures proposed and to consider their possible reaction. One speaker declared in the name of God that he would never submit to the law of the Asiatic Ordinance. This startled Gandhi, for whom the solemn religious vow, taken in the name of God, was of absolute seriousness. He had expected the meeting simply to pass a resolution. But he recognized that a solemn vow might be far more effective. First, however, he had to ensure that all those present fully understood what was to be done. He rose and addressed the meeting:

> I know that pledges and vows are, and should be, taken on rare occasions. A man who takes a vow every now and then is sure to stumble. . . Everyone must search his own inner heart, and if the inner voice assures him that he has the requisite strength to carry him through, then only should he pledge himself and then only will his pledge bear fruit.[13]

He took care to warn people about the possible consequences of a vow not to obey the Ordinance if it should become law.

> We may have to go to jail, where we may be insulted. We may have to go hungry and suffer extreme heat or cold. Hard labour may be imposed upon us. We may be flogged by rude warders. We may be fined heavily. . . Opulent today, we may be reduced to abject poverty tomorrow. We may be deported. Suffering from starvation and similar hardships in jail, some of us may fall ill or even die.

In spite of the warnings, however, all those who were present took an oath not to submit to the Ordinance if it became law. This marked the beginning of programmes of non-violent resistance and non-co-operation led by Gandhiji.

Indian Opinion was used to make known facts about the proposed legislation and the way in which the leaders of the Indian community intended to respond. At first Gandhi was inclined to use the phrase 'passive resistance' to describe the response they had agreed upon. But he decided that the expression had serious drawbacks.

'As the struggle advanced, the phrase "passive resistance" gave rise to confusion and it appeared shameful to permit this great struggle to be known by an English name.' So the columns of *Indian Opinion* were used to launch a competition. What word or phrase best described the campaign of non-violent resistance on which they were launched? It was Maganlal Gandhi whose entry in the competition found most favour with Gandhiji. He suggested *sadagraha*, or 'firmness or force in a good cause'.[14] Gandhi thought the expression was nearly what he wanted. After some thought he altered the word to *satyagraha*, which literally means 'the force of truth'.

> Truth (*satya*) implies love, and firmness (*agraha*) engenders and therefore serves as a synonym for force. I thus began to call the Indian movement 'Satyagraha', that is to say, the Force which is born of Truth and Love or non-violence, and gave up the use of the phrase 'passive resistance'. . . .

Gandhi interpreted passive resistance as a weapon to be used by the weak, and so indeed it had been explained to him. *Satyagraha*, as he conceived it, was to be a weapon of strength. Only those who were spiritually strong would be able to use the weapon of *satyagraha*; only those who were free of cowardice, and absolutely convinced of the right of their cause, could be genuine *satyagrahis*. For *satyagraha* involved the acceptance of suffering for oneself, and the desire of good for one's adversary. 'Satyagraha postulates the conquest of the adversary by suffering in one's own person.'[15]

Satyagraha for Gandhi involved a ruthless regard for honesty, a fearless desire to right wrong, and an attempt to understand an opponent's point of view. He frequently contrasted the 'violence of the weak' with the 'non-violence of the strong', believing *satyagraha* to be a weapon which could be employed effectively only by those who were trained and courageous.

The basis for the notion of *satyagraha* was made up of several elements. It included a practical application of ahimsa as Gandhi had learned it in Gujarat. It included the idea of *nishkama karma*, of duty for duty's sake, as it is taught in the *Bhagavad Gita*. And it included the inspiration that Gandhi had received from writers in the West and from the Sermon on the Mount. Writing many years later in a letter to American friends, Gandhi said:

> . . . you have given me a teacher in Thoreau, who furnished through his essay on the 'Duty of Civil Disobedience' scientific confirmation of what I was doing in South Africa. Great Britain gave me Ruskin, whose *Unto This Last* transformed me overnight from a lawyer and city-dweller into a rustic living away from Durban on a farm, three miles from the nearest railway station; and Russia gave me in Tolstoy a teacher who furnished a reasoned basis for my non-violence. He blessed my movement when it was still in its infancy and of whose wonderful possibilities I had yet to learn.[16]

The *satyagraha* movement in South Africa emerged against a background of events which had provided the Indian community with some hope after the initial shock of the proposed legislation. But the hopes plummeted when the strength of the forces arraigned against the Transvaal Indians became apparent.

A deputation of Indians from South Africa, including Gandhi, sailed to England in October 1906 to make presentations before the British Government. In London Lord Elgin was swayed by the arguments presented to him – although there is no evidence that the threat of pressure from the Indian community influenced him – and he decided not to recommend the implementation of the Ordinance. The decision that the Transvaal act 'would not be proceeded with at present' was announced in the Commons by Winston Churchill on 3 December 1906.[17]

In 1906 the Transvaal was still a Crown Colony. But on 1 January 1907 'responsible government' was conferred on the Transvaal, and this degree of greater independence enabled the Transvaal Government to pass a form of the Indian Registration Act in March 1907.[18]

The Indian community felt betrayed by the British Government and especially resented that aspect of the legislation which required fingerprinting and the carrying of certificates of identification by Indians.

The Transvaal also passed the Immigrants Restriction Act (Act 15 of 1907) which provided that any person unable to write out in 'characters of a European language' an application to enter the colony would be deemed a prohibited immigrant.[19]

The legislation clearly aimed to prevent Indians from entering the Transvaal, imposing restrictions upon them which did not apply to Europeans, and ensuring the close control of Indians already in the Transvaal. Here was an embryo of Pass Laws and other legislation of apartheid in the South Africa of post-World War Two. Gandhi and the Indian leaders recognized the nature of the legislation and the need to resist it. So the *satyagraha* campaign in South Africa began.

In response to the appeals of Gandhi, issued chiefly through the columns of *Indian Opinion*, less than five per cent of Indians registered. The Government responded nervously to this lack of co-operation.

The first test of the *satyagrahis'* nerve came at the end of December 1907, when some of the leaders of the Indian community were ordered to appear in court to show cause why, having failed to register, they should not be deported from the Transvaal.[20] Gandhi was one of those brought to court, and he was sentenced to two months simple imprisonment. For him it was the first of many experiences of prison, and he appears to have found it hard to endure the transition from respected lawyer and community leader to common prisoner.

After only two weeks, however, the government suggested a compromise to encourage registration. The proposal was that Asians in the Transvaal should register voluntarily; Gandhi was led to understand that if this happened, then the Indian Registration Act would be repealed. On 30 January, having agreed to this suggestion, Gandhi was freed from prison. He later suggested that in his agreement with the government's proposal he was expressing the beauty of compromise which he regarded as an important part of the spirit of *satyagraha*. But he still had many political lessons to learn. As time went by it became clear that the Act would not be repealed, and that Gandhi and Smuts had different perceptions of the understanding that was thought to exist between them. Gandhi's agreement to registration appeared to have been a bad error of judgment.

The *satyagraha* campaign had to go on. At a meeting in Johannesburg in August 1908 Asians burned their registration certificates and their trading licences. Gandhi was imprisoned again between October and December 1908 for refusing to produce his certificate of registration on returning to the Transvaal after a visit to Natal. But by this time Gandhi was less upset by imprisonment. Indeed, he appears to have become convinced of the value to his cause of *satyagrahis* allowing themselves to be imprisoned or actively courting imprisonment.

> The conscious breaking of the laws by a whole community and the demand by the transgressors that they be allowed to pay the maximum penalty was so novel and foreign to the bureaucratic mind that it tended to produce panic.[21]

The opposition of the Indian community to the Government's policy and their determination to resist was indicated by a public meeting at which more than 2,000 Indians burned the certificates they had taken out. This attracted welcome publicity to their cause.

'The reporters of English newspapers present at the meeting were profoundly impressed with the whole scene and gave graphic descriptions of the meetings in their papers,' wrote Gandhi.[22] The Johannesburg correspondent of the London *Daily Mail* compared the burning of the certificates with the Boston Tea Party. The cause of the Indians was beginning to attract wider public attention, although at this stage the government did not respond to the provocation.

Later the *satyagrahis* provoked reaction in two ways. They organized the entry into the Transvaal of Natal Indians, in contradiction of the provisions of the Transvaal Immigrants Restriction Bill of 1907; and they encouraged members of the Indian community to engage in street trading without possession of the licences which could only be obtained on production of a registration certificate.[23]

The punishments which could be imposed for the deliberate offences of the *satyagrahis* included fines, imprisonment, and deportation. At first, deportations that were ordered only resulted in people being taken to the borders of the Transvaal. But later the Transvaal Government began to send offenders back to India. This was a dire punishment, as it involved the forfeiture of property and livelihood in South Africa, and sometimes was applied to Indian residents in South Africa who had never lived in India. The policy of deportation had a more serious effect on the morale of the *satyagrahis* than other punishments, and as a consequence, said Gandhi, 'only the real fighters remained'.[24]

However, many Indians went to prison in a determined resistance to the Transvaal Acts, and their courage and perseverance attracted attention within and outside South Africa.

The imprisonment of *satyagrahis* led to practical problems for the leaders of the movement. They had to face the problems of how families were to be cared for while the breadwinners were in prison. Gandhi saw that it would be too expensive to try to meet the normal living expenses of individual families, and the need for a centre where such families could be gathered together and looked after more cheaply became apparent. In 1911 Hermann Kallenbach, a German architect and a supporter of Gandhi, purchased a 1,100 acre farm twenty-one miles from Johannesburg, and offered it rent-free to Gandhi as a settlement for the families of imprisoned *satyagrahis*. This was to become 'Tolstoy Farm', where Gandhi was able to establish a useful centre for the resistance movement, to care for the families of *satyagrahis*, and to carry further the experiments in community living he had derived from Ruskin.

In March 1913 a new issue was added to the causes for which the non-violent resisters were struggling. A legal judgment held that the only marriages which were valid in South Africa were those celebrated by Christian rites and registered by the Registrar of Marriages. This suggested that marriages conducted according to Hindu and Muslim customs were not regarded as legal. The Indian community was deeply concerned about this and Gandhi, who had resolutely refused to add additional issues to those for which they were campaigning, agreed that this was too important to be left outside the concern of the *satyagraha* movement.

The marriage issue also brought Indian women fully into the struggle. Women became *satyagrahis*, several were sentenced to imprisonment, and one died as a result of treatment received in prison. Public interest was aroused in a new way by the participation of women, and Gandhi wrote,

> These events stirred the heart of the Indians not only in South Africa but also in the motherland to its very depths.[25]

The last great event of the South African *satyagraha* movement originated outside the Transvaal. In association with Indian demands in South Africa generally, Indians working in the coal mines in Natal went on strike. The employers cut off electricity and water supply to the company-owned housing in which the miners lived. Gandhi, visiting the area, realized that the men could not hold out long under those conditions. They were also without any kind of strike pay. How could the Indian leadership provide for their housing and upkeep? Gandhi's solution to the problem was both ingenious and politically astute. He decided to organize a march of the strikers from Newcastle, in Natal, to the borders of the Transvaal, thirty-six miles away. Once the strikers crossed into the Transvaal they would become illegal immigrants under the laws which the *satyagrahis* were contesting. Either the government would have to give way on the issue of the free movement of Indians between different states in South Africa, or they would have to imprison, and so feed and house, the men.

On 13 November 1913 Gandhi led the march out of Newcastle, followed by 2,037 men, 127 women, and 57 children.[26] The march attracted a great deal of publicity outside as well as within South Africa, and created widespread sympathy for the cause of the Indians. When they reached the Transvaal, Gandhi and other leaders were imprisoned. The authorities then attempted to turn Gandhi's tactics back on him by returning the marchers to Natal by train, and then imprisoning them in the compounds of their own mines. The mines were cordoned off with barbed wire and declared to be outposts of Dundee and Newcastle prisons. European mine staff were appointed warders, and they attempted to force the men back to work. The labourers refused, and many were whipped and beaten. News of all this reached India, however, and aroused widespread indignation. The *satyagrahis* had scored a victory through the influence of the march and its consequences on public opinion. Gandhi wrote:

> All India was deeply stirred and the South African question became the burning topic of the day.[27]

Even the Viceroy of India, Lord Hardinge, criticized the Government of South Africa in a speech he made in Madras, in spite of the strong tradition that colonial governments did not comment on each other's affairs.

Public opinion outside South Africa had become too strong to be ignored any longer, and South Africa's position within the Empire rendered it amenable to pressure from Britain and India. The *satyagraha* campaign had done its work in creating a climate of opinion in which the government felt obliged to repeal some of the legislation against the Indian community. In 1914 the Indian Relief Bill was passed, validating Indian marriages, and abolishing the annual licence of £3 for those indentured labourers who chose to stay in South Africa.

On 18 July 1914 Gandhi finally left South Africa, sailing for England on a roundabout journey back to India. He felt that his work in South Africa had come to a successful conclusion, and he was especially convinced that in the *satyagraha* struggle he had forged a technique and a set of attitudes which could be of lasting significance.

> . . . had it not been for this great struggle and for the sufferings which many Indians invited upon their devoted heads, the Indians today would have been hounded out of South Africa . . . the victory achieved by Indians in South Africa more or less served as a shield for Indian emigrants in other parts of the British Empire who, if they are suppressed, will be suppressed thanks to the absence of Satyagraha.[28]

6

Non-Violence and Civil Disobedience in India

On his return to India, Gandhi sought to establish a base for the kind of community life he had experienced at Tolstoy Farm. On 25 May 1915, he and a number of companions founded the Satyagraha Ashram near Ahmedabad, in Gujarat. There, in the heart of a very traditional Hindu area, he continued to experiment with the ideas he had learned and practised in South Africa. An early crisis was created at the Satyagraha Ashram when a family of untouchables asked to join the community. Gandhi made quite clear to his supporters and the public that untouchability would not be practised in his ashram. But the progress he had made in South Africa towards the weakening of caste exclusiveness had not been matched in India, and certainly not in Gujarat. Some of the local people who had welcomed the establishment of the ashram now changed their minds about the desirability of Gandhi's presence and influence in their midst. His financial sponsors withdrew their support. Even some of the members of the ashram and of Gandhi's own family had their doubts about the wisdom of ignoring caste feelings about social mixing with untouchables.[1] Gandhi remained sure of the correctness of his policy, and stood firm. Soon another financial backer came forward, and it was accepted that the Gandhian ashram was a place where caste Hindus and untouchables would draw water from the same wells and eat food from a common kitchen. Gandhi felt that his firm stand on this issue helped to change the attitudes of many Hindus to caste exclusiveness.[2]

Meanwhile, Gandhi's contacts with South Africa continued to be strong, and not unnaturally he remained closely involved with further developments there. Before he could turn his attention fully to affairs in India, there was one remaining issue to be cleared up in connection with South Africa. Although much had been achieved in improving the position of Indians in South Africa, there remained one factor which Gandhi and others felt was a clear impediment to full freedom for Indians there. The practice of Indians going to South Africa as indentured labour still continued. Gandhi made his contribution to the efforts to end the indenture system. He had discussions with the government in India and with the Viceroy, and he travelled the country addressing meetings on the issue of indentured labour. The publicity these activities attracted helped to put pressure on the government, and on 31 July 1917, the Government of India announced an end to indentured emigration.[3]

Gandhi gradually began to be more involved in Indian politics, but his introduction to political activity in India was through a number of campaigns at local level to win a measure of justice for workers. The reputation he had made in South Africa had made him well-known in India, where he was particularly regarded as a champion of the oppressed and underprivileged. People started to call on him for help.

Gandhi's campaigning in India began far away from Gujarat, in the state of Bihar. He responded to an appeal for help from the indigo planters in the area of Champaran. The peasants felt that they were badly exploited by the system which demanded that three out of every twenty parts of the land they cultivated should be planted with indigo, grown for the profit of the landlords. Growing indigo was unproductive so far as local food needs were concerned, and it was a dirty job which left the peasants stained with irremovable marks of their labour.

Gandhi travelled to Champaran and began to make his own enquiries. But his presence in the area was objected to by the landlords, who persuaded the civil authorities to issue an order to Gandhi to leave the area. Gandhi refused to leave, was taken to court, pleaded guilty, and made a statement before the magistrate about the reasons for his presence in the area. He also took the precaution of sending a wire to the Viceroy and to a number of his friends to ensure that the action of the local authorities and the cause of the peasants should be more widely known. When the time came for the magistrate to pronounce sentence, he announced instead that the case against Gandhi was withdrawn on the orders of the Lieutenant Governor. The action of the landlords had backfired, and was a great help to Gandhi.

The country thus had its first direct object-lesson in Civil Disobedience. The affair was fully discussed both locally and in the press, and my inquiry got unexpected publicity.[4]

With the assistance of a number of *vakils*, Gandhi then took statements from many of the peasants. He was surprised to discover how great was their poverty and how deep their ignorance. He sent for helpers to come to the area and establish basic schools in the villages, to teach hygiene as well as reading and writing. With the help of Dr Dev, of the Servants of India Society, he also promoted basic medical work in the area.

The activity of Gandhi and his helpers led the Lieutenant Governor to set up a Committee of Enquiry, on which Gandhi agreed to serve. The Committee recommended the ending of the *tinkathia* system, by which three parts out of every twenty had to be planted with indigo for the landlords, and ordered a refund of part of the profits that had been made from the practice. Gandhi returned victorious from Champaran, having laid important foundations for his future work in India and having secured a reputation as friend and advocate for the poor and oppressed.[5]

He was then asked to intervene on behalf of mill-workers in Ahmedabad. The issue here was of a very different kind. Mill-workers had been attracted to Ahmedabad during the war years when the cotton industry flourished. They were paid good wages, although prices had also been forced up by wartime conditions. In 1917 an outbreak of plague sent many workers back to their villages, where they hoped to escape infection. In order to hold their employees, the mill-owners paid a special plague bonus of seventy-five per cent. Once that particular threat had subsided, they proposed to end the subsidy, and announced that the seventy-five per cent would not be paid after 15 February 1918. The workers demanded a rise of fifty per cent to compensate for the lost bonus, and the employers offered twenty per cent. Feelings ran high, there was a lock-out, and a strike which Gandhi supported.[6]

Conscious of his responsibilities in the matter, Gandhi set out four conditions of a successful strike: never resort to violence; never molest blacklegs; never depend on alms; remain firm, however long the strike lasts, and earn money by other honest means. Daily meetings were held at which Gandhi exhorted the workers. But after two weeks he detected a weakening of resolve among the strikers. Some, unsure of success, thought they had better return to work; others were being led by their frustration to violent reaction. Gandhi wondered what he could do to maintain the enthusiasm of the strikers and to preserve the atmosphere of moral integrity which he regarded as so important a part of the struggle. Then he stumbled upon the idea of a fast. Fasting was to become an important weapon in Gandhi's Indian campaigns. 1918 in Ahmedabad was the first time he used it as a political weapon.

> One morning – it was at a mill-hands' meeting – while I was still groping and unable to see my way clearly, the light came to me. Unbidden and all by themselves the words came to my lips: 'Unless the strikers rally,' I declared to the meeting, 'and continue the strike till a settlement is reached, or till they leave the mills altogether, I will not touch any food.'[7]

Gandhi claimed that he was not striking against the mill-owners, with whom he had previously had friendly relationships, but of course his action put considerable pressure on them. The fast also created great enthusiasm among the strikers. After a strike of twenty-one days a settlement was reached on the basis of a compromise between the demands of the mill-workers and the offer of the employers.

The third major incident of 1917–18 for Gandhi was the Kheda *satyagraha*. Conditions in Kheda, or Kaira, in Gujarat, were approaching famine. Under the Land Revenue Rules, if a crop was worth four annas or less, the revenue assessment levied on the tenant-farmers was to be waived. The official figures produced for Kheda that year claimed that the crop was worth more than four annas. The workers in the fields claimed that the crop was worth less. Gandhi was again called upon to help. His presence ensured that the local issue became a matter of public notice, and his genius for compromise suggested a solution. The cultivators themselves at first resolved not to pay the full revenue for the year, even if their lands should become forfeit. They then went on to suggest that:

> Should the Government . . . agree to suspend collection of the second instalment of the assessment throughout the district such amongst us as are in a position to pay will pay up the whole or the balance of the revenue that may be due.[8]

The compromise was accepted by the authorities, and the campaign came to an end. But Gandhi was not entirely happy with the outcome, which did not seem to him to have gained enough for the peasants or to have expressed sufficiently clearly the ideals of *satyagraha*.

... the end was far from making me feel happy, inasmuch as it lacked the grace with which the termination of every Satyagraha campaign ought to be accompanied. The Collector carried on as though he had done nothing by way of a settlement. The poor were to be granted suspension, but hardly any got the benefit of it. . . . The end of a Satyagraha campaign can be described as worthy, only when it leaves the Satyagrahis stronger and more spirited than they are at the beginning.[9]

Gandhi did acknowledge, however, that the Kheda *satyagraha* marked an awakening among the Gujarati peasants and 'the beginning of their true political education'. He judged that the campaign had been important for the way in which it had brought his sympathizers into contact with the peasants and increased among educated people an understanding of the problems of the poor. In spite of his disappointment, Gandhi felt that the Kheda *satyagraha* had given new vigour to public life in Gujarat.

At this time, during the last months of the Great War, the paradoxes of Gandhi's attitudes to non-violence were emphasized by his participation in a conference on the war effort called by the Viceroy. As a result of the conference, Gandhi agreed to take part in a recruiting campaign to encourage the enlistment of Indian soldiers. He found the work unrewarding, and even expressed some surprise at the different reception he received as he toured on behalf of the war effort from that given him when he had appeared in his role of non-violent fighter against injustice and oppression. Villagers readily recognized the contradiction between his stated policy of *ahimsa* and his support of the allied war effort. But as in South Africa at the time of the Boer War, Gandhi was persuaded that the British Empire provided a framework within which justice could be secured for subject peoples. Only by supporting the Empire in times of need, he believed, could the people of India justify their demands for justice at the hands of the Empire. He also believed that the expression of good will and support which would be shown by Indian participation in the war effort would be matched by reform and concessions on their behalf after the war. In a letter to the Viceroy, he wrote:

I would make India offer all her able-bodied sons as a sacrifice to the Empire at its critical moment, and I know that India, by this very act, would become the most favoured partner in the Empire, and racial distinctions would become a thing of the past.[10]

This attitude revealed Gandhi's limited knowledge of the war situation in Europe, although in this he was little different from millions of private individuals whose understanding of the war while it was in progress was dependent upon Government propaganda. But Gandhi also seemed to have rather naive expectations of what might be expected from the British Government once the war was over. Certainly Gandhi's response to the Viceroy's appeal for help with the war effort demonstrated once again that Gandhi's *ahimsa* did not involve a thoroughgoing pacifism. In matters of political reform he believed non-violence to be important as a principle, as well as being the most effective technique available in the Indian situation. But he did not apply the same principle of non-violence to a distant war in Europe. ·

Gandhi's early involvement in civil disobedience in India came to a climax with the traumatic events which surrounded the introduction of the Rowlatt Acts in 1919. In February of that year a Bill was introduced into the Imperial Legislative Council which proposed giving the Government powers to deal with areas officially labelled as subversive. The powers included summary arrest, trial without jury, and the holding of legal proceedings in camera if the judge thought necessary. The proposals aroused strong feelings and widespread opposition among Indian politicians. Every Indian member of the Imperial Legislative Council opposed the measures, but they were carried none the less. The passage of the Bill exposed the severe limitations of the policy of co-operation by Indian politicians with the Government of the Viceroy in the expectation that gradual reform would be achieved.[11] There was a great outcry in the Indian Press. Gandhi, like others, was indignant at the draconian measures of the Rowlatt Acts; he also seized the opportunity it afforded him of taking a more central position on the stage of Indian politics. He wrote:

> I feel I can no longer render peaceful obedience to the laws of a power that is capable of such a piece of devilish legislation as these two bills, and I would not hesitate to invite those who think with me to join in the struggle.[12]

At a meeting at Gandhi's ashram at Ahmedabad a *satyagraha sabha* (or organization) was formed to fight the Rowlatt Acts, and a *satyagraha* pledge formulated for those who wished to join in active but non-violent opposition to the Government.[13] The pledge was in the following terms:

Being conscientiously of the opinion that the Rowlatt Bills

. . . are unjust, subversive of the principle of liberty and justice, and destructive of the elementary rights of individuals on which the safety of the community as a whole and the State itself is based, we solemnly affirm that, in the event of these Bills becoming law and until they are withdrawn, we shall refuse civilly to obey these laws and such other laws as a Committee to be hereafter appointed may think fit, and we further affirm that in this struggle we will faithfully follow truth and refrain from violence to life, person or property.[14]

Gandhi's initiative at this time was not universally welcomed by Indian politicians, however. He had strong support in his native Gujarat and in Bombay, but outside those areas his political power was weak. Annie Besant, at this time an important leader of the Indian National Congress, was reluctant to follow Gandhi's lead and perhaps a little jealous of his growing influence. On 2 March 1919 the Indian non-official members of the Imperial Legislative Council signed a manifesto opposing Gandhi's moves:

While strongly condemning the Rowlatt Bills as drastic and unnecessary and while we think we must oppose them to the end, we disapprove of the passive resistance movement started as a protest against them and dissociate ourselves from it in the best interests of the country, especially in view of the reforms proposals which are about to be laid before Parliament.[15]

The idea of deliberate civil disobedience was still a difficult one for leading politicians to accept. As it transpired, the Gandhian concepts of civil disobedience as expressed in the pledge were little understood by people generally.

But the *satyagraha* movement went ahead. Gandhi proposed a *hartal*, as a major public demonstration of disapproval with the Rowlatt Acts. A *hartal* is a general closure of shops, businesses, transport services for a limited period (often just one day) in order to register protest or disapproval. Initially the *hartal* was proposed for 30 March, although the date was changed to 6 April when it became apparent that preparations could not be made in time. Due to poor communications, however, the *hartal* went ahead on the 30 March in Delhi, where it was accompanied by some violence. Congress leaders were still uncertain about the wisdom of the *satyagraha* movement, or perhaps of affording Gandhi such opportunities for national leadership. On 3 April, Annie Besant actually visited Bombay in order to disuade people from joining the *hartal*.[16]

On 6 April the *hartal* went ahead. In Bombay it was successful. About four-fifths of the shops shut and very few taxis ran. On the other side of the country, in Bengal, the *hartal* was observed in the big cities of Dacca and Calcutta, but little noticed elsewhere. Similarly, in the south it was observed in Madras city, but had little impact in the countryside. The *hartal* was well organized in the United Provinces, although there too it was predominantly urban. And in the Punjab it was almost universal in all the large towns.[17] In Bombay the *hartal* was accompanied by other activities. One of the problems facing Gandhi and his supporters had been the fact that whilst the closure of shops might be a protest of sorts, it was not an act of civil disobedience. No law, and certainly nothing connected with the Rowlatt Acts, demanded that shops should be kept open. What else could the *satyagrahis* do that would constitute civil disobedience? Gandhi hit upon two ideas in Bombay. One was to encourage people to distil salt from sea water, in defiance of the Salt Tax laws. The other was to sell in the streets copies of two of Gandhi's books, *Hind Swaraj* and *Sarvodaya*, both of which had been proscribed.[18] The books sold well, but the police turned a blind eye, thus spoiling the point of the demonstration.

On 8 April, Gandhi took a train for Amritsar, intending to encourage the demonstrations that were going strongly in the Punjab. The Governor of the Punjab, Sir Michael O'Dwyer, regarding Gandhi simply as a trouble-maker, was determined that he should not enter the Punjab, and on his orders Gandhi was taken from the train by the police and escorted back to Bombay, where he was released. The fact that Gandhi genuinely believed in the principle of non-violence, and therefore would aid the civil authorities by urging the crowds to refrain from violence, had presumably not occurred to O'Dwyer. And it was in the Punjab that the most bloodshed occurred, with the infamous massacre at Jallianwalla Bagh, an incident that stirred the hearts of millions of Indians, and has remained ever since a memorial to the cost of the struggle for independence.

In Amritsar there had been a widespread observance of *hartal* and a number of demonstrations with some violence. The British authorities were clearly nervous, and correspondence among the British leadership in Amritsar clearly shows that some of them had in mind the analogy of the Indian Revolt of 1857, suspecting that the unrest of early April might be the precursor of a nation-wide rising against the British and virtual civil war.[19] On 10 April news of Gandhi's arrest and the arrest of two Punjabi politicians sparked off mob violence in Amritsar. The local military commander, General Dyer, announced martial law, although it is doubtful whether many people would have had the opportunity of seeing the announcement. The imposition of martial law included a ban on public meetings and a curfew. Local Indian leaders had organized a public meeting, and in defiance of the martial law orders the meeting went ahead. Some 10,000 people crowded into Jallianwalla Bagh, a public park surrounded by buildings with only a narrow gateway to provide access. General Dyer led his troops to the Bagh, his mind quite made up on the necessity of acting firmly in order to prevent a general uprising against the British throughout India. He ordered his troops to open fire on the unarmed and peaceful crowd, without warning and without any opportunity for the crowd to disperse. The geography of Jallianwalla Bagh made it impossible for people to escape once the firing had started. Clearly the object was not to disperse the crowd, and orders to the soldiers were to fire at, rather than above, the people.[20] After ten minutes of firing, General Dyer led his troops away, leaving the dead and dying in the Jallianwalla Bagh as dusk fell and the curfew made it difficult for helpers to reach them. The official count gave a death-toll of 400, although a later Congress estimate suggested a figure of 1,000. Many more were injured. Whilst the blame for this appalling massacre lay at the feet of General Dyer and his troops, there were Indian politicians who could point to the tragedy as an indication of the futility of *satyagraha*.

Meanwhile there had been riots in Ahmedabad, and martial law had been declared there. Gandhi travelled to Ahmedabad from Bombay. There he found,

> The people were terror-stricken. They had indulged in acts of violence and were being made to pay for them with interest.[21]

A public meeting was held in Ahmedabad on 13 April. Gandhi recalled:

> Addressing the meeting I tried to bring home to the people the sense of their wrong, declared a penitential fast of three days for myself, appealed to the people to go on a similar fast for a day, and suggested to those who had been guilty of acts of violence to confess their guilt.[22]

From Ahmedabad, Gandhi went on to nearby Nadiad, where at a public meeting he described the launching of a premature *satyagraha* campaign as a 'Himalayan miscalculation'. That phrase came to be associated with Gandhi's influence on events not only in Gujarat and Bombay but also in the Punjab. But the miscalculation helped Gandhi, and others, to identify the groundwork that was necessary before a successful and non-violent campaign could be launched. Gandhi wrote:

> Before one can be fit for the practice of civil disobedience one must have rendered a willing and respectful obedience to the state laws. . . A Satyagraha obeys the laws of society intelligently and of his own free will, because he considers it to be his sacred duty to do so. It is only when a person has thus obeyed the laws of society scrupulously that he is in a position to judge as to which particular laws are good and which unjust and iniquitous. Only then does the right accrue to him of the civil disobedience of certain laws in well-defined circumstances. My error lay in my failure to observe this necessary limitation. I had called on the people to launch upon civil disobedience before they had thus qualified themselves for it, and this mistake seemed to me of Himalayan magnitude.[23]

Gandhi concluded that before starting civil disobedience on a mass scale it would be necessary to train volunteers thoroughly, so that they in turn could instil the ideals and techniques of *satyagraha* in the mass of people. It was particularly the ideals of *satyagraha* that Gandhi wanted to communicate. He wished people to understand his own firm commitment to truth and his convictions that a struggle in a righteous cause must ultimately prevail. He wanted to communicate his own beliefs about the essential connections between cause and effect, means and ends. The means one used to struggle for justice were to him as important as the end itself, for if the means were corrupt or violent, then so would the free state turn out to be corrupt and violent when once established.[24]

How was Gandhi to convey these often subtle ideas to a large number of people? His chief means were his publications, particularly the English weekly *Young India* and the Gujarati *Navajivan*, now converted from a monthly to a weekly, and both published from Ahmedabad. Week after week Gandhi poured out his ideas in these papers.

Meanwhile the *satyagraha* campaign against the Rowlatt Acts was shorn of those ingredients that seemed to lead to violence, and on 18 April 1919 Gandhi called off the civil disobedience part of the *satyagraha* programme. Although a failure so far as the intended results were concerned, the civil disobedience of April

1919 had taught Gandhi much. Perhaps even more important, it had led Gandhi from his concern with local issues to a major role on the all-India political scene.

Judith Brown wrote of this period:

The Rowlatt Satyagraha, as a political campaign on the lines which its author conceived, was a manifest failure. It did not obtain its object, the repeal of the Rowlatt Act. It erupted into violence, though its essence was intended to be non-violence. It petered out miserably in the summer months of 1919 instead of becoming the constructive campaign laying the foundations of true Swaraj which Gandhi had envisaged. Nevertheless, as Gandhi's first essay in all-India leadership it was remarkably instructive to those who could read it correctly, since it showed both the strengths and weaknesses of the Mahatma in politics.[25]

In addition to putting Gandhi firmly at the centre of the Indian political stage, the events of 1919 also enabled him to take a leading role in the Indian National Congress, and to persuade Congress to adopt a policy of non-cooperation. It was already clear that Gandhi's approach to Indian politics was essentially different from that of Western-educated leaders. His deliberate acts of identification with the poor people of the villages, symbolized by his simple dress and his carefully cultivated life-style and enhanced by his religious and moral earnestness, gave him an all-India appeal denied to other politicians. He also saw that the power of the British Raj depended upon co-operation from the Indian people, and in advocating non-cooperation he believed that he could make the process of government impossible for the British.

Gandhi widened his concerns, and his political base, from mid-1919 by supporting Muslim agitation to defend the office of the Khalifat after Turkey's defeat in the First World War. Indian Muslims feared that the collapse of Muslim powers in the Middle East would weaken Muslim political influence in India. Three claims were made by Muslims: that the Khalifat should retain sufficient temporal power to defend the faith of Islam; that the geographical centres of Islam in Arabia should remain under Muslim control; and that the Khalifat should retain control of Muslim sanctuaries. In supporting Indian Muslims as they participated in this campaign Gandhi saw himself involved in the defence of a principle, and also recognized the ways in which association with the Muslims could help the cause of Hindu-Muslim unity. The importance of this cause for Gandhi's political standing is well summarized by Judith Brown:

The Khilafat movement from early 1919 until the inauguration of non-cooperation on 1 August 1920 was the context of Gandhi's rapid emergence as an all-India political leader who was markedly different from the politicians who had previously dominated India's political world. During the Rowlatt satyagraha Gandhi had advised specific and limited types of civil disobedience by a picked group of satyagrahis: by mid-1920 his participation in the Khilafat movement had led him to try to organize a mass movement of political protest, taking the form of withdrawal of cooperation from the government. This new departure was the complete antithesis of the limited politics of the Congress and older Muslim League leaders. It resumed the participation in politics of far greater numbers from a much wider social, religious and geographical range than before. It also undermined the basic assumption on which conventional politics rested, namely that the aims of the tiny fraction of the India population who made up the political nation were most likely to be reached by judicious cooperation with the raj.[26]

A second issue which brought Gandhi to the centre of Congress politics in 1919 and 1920 arose out of the Jallianwalla Bagh massacre. Widespread protests at General Dyer's action led the Government to set up a Committee of Enquiry, chaired by Lord Hunter, in October 1919. The Committee reported in May 1920, and the majority found in favour of the Governor of the Punjab, O'Dwyer, and General Dyer. Gandhi strongly condemned the Hunter report, which he described as 'page after page of thinly disguised official whitewash',[27] and he supported pleas for the impeachment of O'Dwyer. The Khilafat campaign and the Punjab enquiry were two issues which aroused great public concern at all levels of society; they were not simply matters of debate among the politically educated.

In spite of the apparent failure of the Rowlatt *satyagraha*, Gandhi could use these two issues to re-assert his claims to lead a non-violent movement of non-cooperation at a national rather than a local level. In April 1920 Gandhi became President of the All-India Home Rule League, in succession to Annie Besant, and this was his first official role in Indian politics. He quickly used the leverage this gave him (and some of his opponents claimed that he acted autocratically). On 1 August he launched a programme of non-cooperation entirely on his own authority. He returned his Zulu and Boer War medals and his Kaiser-i-Hind gold medal to the Viceroy with a letter explaining why he could no longer cooperate with the British Raj. At the beginning of July the Non-Cooperation Movement had issued a statement through the columns of *Young India* explaining what would be involved in a programme of non-cooperation:

> Should non-co-operation become necessary the Committee has decided upon the following as part of the first stage:
> 1. Surrender of all titles of honour and honorary offices.
> 2. Non-participation in Government loans.
> 3. Suspension by lawyers of practice and settlement of civil disputes by private arbitration.
> 4. Boycott of Government schools by parents.
> 5. Boycott of the reformed councils.
> 6. Non-participation in Government parties, and such other functions.
> 7. Refusal to accept any civil or military post, in Mesopotamia, or to offer as Units for the army especially for services in the Turkish territories now being administered in violation of pledges.
> 8. Vigorous prosecution of Swadeshi inducing the people at the time of this national and religious awakening, to appreciate their primary duty to their country, by being satisfied with its own productions and manufactures.[28]

Not surprisingly, such sweeping condemnation of participation in the ordinary political and civil life of the nation did not win immediate support from other politicians, many of whom in any case were angered by the peremptory way in which Gandhi had launched his programme.

In September a special session of the Congress met in Calcutta, and had the opportunity to debate the non-cooperation programme. Against the advice of much of the Congress leadership, Gandhi's motion proposing non-cooperation was carried. At a full session of Congress at Nagpur in December the Calcutta proposal was reaffirmed in the following terms:

> This Congress reaffirms the resolution passed at its last Special Session advising non-violent progressive non-cooperation with the Government for the purpose of rectification of the Khilafat and the Punjab wrongs and attaining Swaraj. . .[29]

Gandhi appeared to believe at this time that a programme of non-cooperation could bring *swaraj*, or self-rule, within a year, although there was no clear understanding among the Congress leaders as to what they meant by *swaraj*, and Gandhi himself was very vague on the subject.[30] In the event this particular phase of non-violent resistance to British rule petered out within a short time. Support for such policies as withdrawal of students from schools and colleges was very limited, Congress politicians themselves were divided or half-hearted about the programme, and there was still far too limited an understanding of the techniques and ideals involved in the Gandhian approach to politics.[31] Violence grew among those involved in the non-cooperation programme, and the campaign was called off after the killing of 22 policemen in the United Provinces in February 1922. In the course of the campaign, however, as many as 30,000 Congress workers had been sent to prison, and in March 1922 Gandhi followed them there.[32] He was arrested on March 10 on a charge of writing seditious articles in *Young India* and was sentenced to six years imprisonment. The non-cooperation movement was at an end.

Gandhi served only twenty-two months of his sentence, being released partly because he needed an operation for appendicitis. Certainly he was much weakened by his prison experience. His *satyagraha* experiment had not produced the results he had expected. During the four years after his release he was engaged very little in major political activity.

His re-introduction of *satyagraha* was occasioned by events in Bardoli, in Gujarat, and was reminiscent of the local campaigns that had brought him to public attention between 1917 and 1919. In 1928 the Government increased the land revenue tax by twenty-eight per cent. The people of Bardoli asked Gandhi to help them to organize against this, and so a civil disobedience campaign was launched.[33] Under Gandhi's leadership the peasants refused to pay the additional tax. The Government retaliated by arresting many of them and by confiscating property. Gandhi's teaching about non-violence seemed this time to be effective. There was no violence; the peasants courageously withstood the pressure exerted upon them, and in the end the Government gave way. The tax increase was rescinded, the prisoners were released, and the property was restored. The experience was an important one for Gandhi, and helped to restore his confidence in his methods. Once more he began to see a role for non-violent resistance in the struggle for independence. The Bardoli campaign, said Gandhi, 'has revived our drooping spirits, it has brought us new hope, it has shown the immense possibilities of mass non-violence practised not from conviction, but like most virtues with most of us as a policy'.[34]

However, it was two more years before Gandhi again launched a national civil disobedience campaign. At the beginning of 1930, Congress opened a campaign for all-out independence, thus resolving a long debate about whether to go for dominion status or complete independence. On 19 February the All India Congress Committee adopted a civil disobedience programme as the most effective way of pursuing their goal. Gandhi was expected to lead the civil disobedience and, indeed, to find the pretext for beginning such a campaign. Bitter experience had shown how difficult it was to launch a successful and well-controlled campaign of civil disobedience. But this time Gandhi found a cause and a method of pursuing it which are a model of non-violent action. He decided on a large-scale public demonstration against the Salt Tax. The tax illustrated the way in which an expensive foreign administration was maintained at least in part by levying taxes on an exceptionally poor population. It was a tax on a commodity regarded by most people as an essential, especially in a hot climate (although Gandhi himself did not normally take salt as part of his strict dietary rule!). And a campaign against the Salt Tax would injure no one, yet gather widespread support.

Gandhi first wrote a letter to Lord Irwin, the Viceroy:

The iniquities (of the tax laws in general and the salt laws in particular) . . . are maintained in order to carry on a foreign administration, demonstrably the most expensive in the world. Take your own salary. . . You are getting over 700 rupees per day against India's average income of less than two annas per day. . . Thus you are getting over five thousand times India's average income . . . a system that provides for such an arrangement deserves to be summarily scrapped. . . nothing but unadulterated non-violence can check the organized violence of the British government. . .

But if you cannot see your way to deal with these evils and my letter makes no appeal to your heart, on the eleventh day of this month, I shall proceed with such co-workers of this ashram as I can take, to disregard the provisions of the law.[35]

Apart from a formal acknowledgement, the Viceroy ignored the letter, and so Gandhi began his march from the ashram in Ahmedabad to Dandi, 240 miles away on the coast.

The marchers made the entire journey on foot, proceeding at a leisurely pace through towns and villages and gathering supporters on the way. Public meetings were held along the route, and great interest was shown in the march by the press. On 5 April the marchers reached Dandi and distilled salt from the sea. The *satyagrahis* had been prepared for violent opposition. They had been prepared for danger, and warned that their participation could endanger their freedom and even their lives. Gandhi himself saw the march as an act of non-violence that could demand the sacrifice of his life. Mehta wrote:

> Gandhi's journey to Dandi was compared by his disciples and followers to Jesus's journey to Jerusalem; many Hindus who could read bought copies of the Bible and read it. Gandhi himself apparently thought that he might have to die in Dandi as Jesus died in Jerusalem.[36]

The *satyagrahis* remained at Dandi, making and selling salt and waiting to see how the Government would react to their calculated breaking of the law. At first the official reaction was cautious, expecting that the movement would gradually fade away. But in other parts of the country people started to emulate the example of the Dandi *satyagrahis*. Deliberate breaking of the law, usually although not always in a non-violent fashion, was becoming popular throughout the country.[37] At last the authorities decided to act. On 5 May the police went to Gandhi's camp in the middle of the night and arrested him. He was sent back to Yeravda prison at Poona, where he had spent nearly two years between 1922 and 1924. The salt *satyagraha* came to an end with the breaking of the monsoon in June 1930.

Another effective part of the campaign against British rule in this period was a boycott of foreign cloth. Gandhi had in the spinning wheel a symbol of the determination of the people to achieve self-dependence; his followers were all encouraged to learn to weave cloth, and the wearing of the coarse off-white *khadi* cloth became a badge of the Gandhian movement. It was logical to accompany that with an effort to dissuade people from buying and selling imported cloth. Judith Brown commented:

> Overall India's imports of cotton manufactures dropped from Rs. 59 crores in 1929–30 to Rs. 25 crores in 1930–31: imports of cotton price-goods contracted from 1,919 million yards valued at Rs. 50 crores to 890 million yards valued at Rs. 20 crores. The slump in world prices, the contraction of good markets for Indian goods and raw material and the consequent decrease in India's purchasing power were partly responsible for a general

decline in India's foreign trade. But in price-goods trade the boycott clearly had a marked effect, since the decline in imports was greater than that of other commodities and affected British goods more than those from any other country.[38]

The civil disobedience movement was to go on. On 1 January 1932 a Congress Working Committee at Bombay passed the following resolution:

Nothing short of complete independence carrying full control over the Defence and External Affairs and Finance . . . can be regarded as satisfactory. . . In the event of a satisfactory response not forthcoming the Working Committee calls upon the nation to resume civil disobedience.[39]

As the movement continued, so its leader came to be regarded with increasing hostility by the authorities. Gandhi was released from Yeravda on 26 January 1931, but was arrested again a year later, on 26 January 1932, and held in custody until 8 May 1933.

The frustrations felt by authorities in having to deal with large numbers of demonstrators was reflected in the increasing use of violence by the police and the charge that civil disobedience must inevitably lead to violence.

One of Mahatma Gandhi's best-known European supporters, C. F. Andrews, wrote a letter to the Government of India in April 1932 complaining about police excesses:

The absurdly simple and obvious fact which I found out in 1919 was this, that the police, however admirable for routine work under strict control, are an impossible weapon to use under emergency ordinances, which put almost unlimited power in their hands. . . Many accounts have reached me of the incident of a woman being stripped naked in Benares. There has also been given me a series of affidavits about similar incidents happening near Anand in Gujerat. . .

Never before, I believe, in British Indian history, have women been imprisoned in large numbers as they are being jailed today. Not only will evil things certainly happen, but stories will pass from mouth to mouth through all the villages of India.[40]

The reply suggested that it was the demonstrators whose activities produced the violence. The Government of India replied:

The results which you apprehend but which, as I shall mention below, are not, I believe, being realized, are precisely the results which the leaders of the civil disobedience movement counted on producing. The whole policy of civil resistance is directed to the end of either paralysing the Government or leading to action which will alienate public opinion. . .

My main point therefore is that it is the deliberate intention of the leaders of the civil disobedience movement to create the conditions against which you warn . . . the responsibility must lie with those who incite women to 'step into the breach', and deliberately resort to the employment of women in order to add to the difficulties of the Government.[41]

The establishment view of Gandhi and of civil disobedience at this time was reflected in the columns of *The Times of India*, which referred to Gandhi in 1930 as 'the man who is leading India to chaos and anarchy', and said that he had given abundant proof that he rejected 'the way of reason in favour of destructive methods'.[42] And commenting on his arrest a few days later, said:

. . . a movement which is professedly non-violent has led as was expected, to acts of violence, which Mr Gandhi is unable to control. . . Mr Gandhi was deliberately leading India to chaos.[43]

Clearly Gandhi was not being arrested for actually fomenting violence. The reaction against him indicated the growing importance of the civil disobedience movement and the threat it posed to continued British rule. *Satyagraha* was making an impact upon the Government.

In 1933 the Home Department of the Government of India felt it necessary to issue a warning to all educational institutions in India aided by the Government telling them not to arrange lectures by Mr Gandhi during his tours in connection with the uplift of untouchables.[44] Even so laudable a social enterprise was to be regarded with suspicion and as politically suspect when propounded by Gandhi.

The widespread violation of laws which the civil disobedience movement came to involve put increasing pressure on the Government. The Governor General issued the following statement in January 1932:

Experience has proved time and again that in this country civil disobedience cannot be carried on without violence and Mr Gandhi himself has spoken of the sacrifice of a million lives. . . It is their (Government of India's) duty to resist, with all their might, forces which would create a state of anarchy and chaos. . .

An issue of hardly less importance is whether a political organization is to be allowed by lawless means to impose its will on the public, large sections of which deny its authority and oppose its intentions.[45]

Antipathetic attitudes to Gandhi were not confined to members of the British establishment in India. There were plenty of people in Britain who thought that there was something distinctly odd about the approach of Gandhi to politics. His dress, his habits of daily life, his apparent simplicity, and his unwavering belief in non-violent methods of resistance marked him out from the current stereotype of the politician. He did not conform, and therefore he was suspect. Winston Churchill remarked how humiliating it was for Britain to see the 'spectacle of this one-time Inner Temple lawyer, now seditious fakir, striding half-naked up the steps of the Viceroy's palace, there to negotiate with the representative of the King-Emperor'.[46]

Gandhi, on his release from prison in 1931, visited London and took part in the Second Round Table Conference, which achieved little except to expose the differences between the British and Indian nationalist leaders and also, perhaps more alarmingly, the differences between Congress, the Muslim League and the princes. After his next period of imprisonment Gandhi called off the civil disobedience movement and was not directly involved in Congress politics for the rest of the 1930s.

With the beginning of the Second World War, Gandhi was again caught up in national affairs. This time his non-violence seemed to be more consistently applied to war than on previous occasions, although he supported hopes of an allied victory. In the first month of the war he wrote in *Harijan*:

> My personal reaction towards this war is one of greater horror than ever before. I was not so disconsolate before as I am today. But the greater horror would prevent me today from becoming the self-appointed recruiting sergeant that I had become during the last war. And yet, strange as it may appear, my sympathies are wholly with the allies.[47]

He was disappointed with the Congress attitude, which implied violent resistance, and this appeared to Gandhi to reveal a basic misunderstanding of the ideal of non-violence he had so long held out before Congress workers.

This is tragic. . . The fact is, however, that our fight has not been one of non-violent resistance of the strong. It has been one of passive resistance of the weak. . .[48]

There was strong reaction within the independence movement against the action of the Viceroy, whose declaration of war on behalf of India was made without any reference to nationalist leaders. If India was to be involved with fighting the war, there had to be a clear understanding of precisely how and when independence was to be granted after the war. Gandhi at first initiated a policy of individual *satyagraha* to press the claim for a decision on independence. This was calculated to put pressure on the Government without presenting them in wartime with all the difficulties and commitment of troops and police which would result from mass *satyagraha*. Over a period of about a year some 23,000 Congress workers were imprisoned, including Jawaharlal Nehru.[49]

In March 1942 Sir Stafford Cripps visited India as an emissary of the British Government in an attempt to work out an acceptable formula for eventual independence. The talks broke down, and in August 1942 Gandhi launched a mass civil disobedience campaign – the 'Quit India' campaign. Congress workers were advised to consider themselves free of British rule. The Government responded firmly, and all the Congress leaders were arrested and imprisoned.

Gandhi was imprisoned on 9 August 1942 and spent the next two years in prison. His main publication, *Harijan*, was banned soon afterwards, and that invaluable record of Gandhi's thought began to appear again only in 1946.

The end of the war brought with it the events which led swiftly to Indian independence, but also witnessed the sad end of *satyagraha* and the death of Gandhi. The Labour Government of Clement Attlee, elected just before the end of the war in 1945, expressed its willingness to negotiate Indian independence as soon as agreement could be reached with the various parties (chiefly the Congress, the Muslim League, and the princes who ruled the Princely States). The Muslim leader Jinnah clearly and consistently demanded a separate homeland for Muslims. Gandhi despaired at this policy, which was a negation of so much that he had worked for in Hindu-Muslim unity since 1919. But neither he nor other Congress leaders could find any way of persuading Jinnah to work for a united India.

In 1946 the Interim Government was established, with a Governor General presiding over an Indian Cabinet, but wrangling over the Constitution that was to be adopted, and especially over the question of partition, continued. In August 1946 Jinnah initiated a direct-action programme for the creation of Pakistan, and a bitter religious war began. The determination of the British Government to force matters to a conclusion in India was made apparent by the declaration of 20 February 1947 stating that India must govern herself by June 1948, whether or not final agreement on a constitution had been reached.[50] This finally persuaded Hindus that with solid Muslim support partition was inevitable. But it did nothing to ease the violence which the prospect of partition had evoked. There was bitter conflict between Muslims and Hindus all across north India, but especially in the areas which were to become the borders between India and Pakistan, in the Punjab and Kashmir in the West, and in Bengal in the East. The cities and towns were more badly affected than the rural areas, but one of the worst outbreaks of violence occurred in the rural area of Noakhali, in Bengal. Noakhali was a predominantly Muslim area, and Hindus living there were savagely attacked. It was remote, with scattered villages, thick jungle, and many rivers.

Gandhi decided to go to Noakhali. Rather than stay near the centres of power and communication, where he felt a helpless witness of events, he chose to go and live among some of the people who were suffering most to try to persuade them to be at peace with each other. The dangers to Gandhi, as the best-known Hindu leader of India, were obvious. But he insisted on going, and took with him a small band of helpers. He toured the villages on foot, preaching his message of non-violence. To many leading politicians Gandhi's behaviour again appeared bizarre. At a moment of great crisis he left the centres of influence and power and buried himself in a remote area, full of danger to himself and his companions. To Gandhi, the action was consistent with his lifetime ideals. It was one of the last great gestures by which he appealed for non-violence.[51]

In the period immediately after independence the violence became even worse, as refugees struggled to cross the new borders that had been established between the Muslim state of Pakistan and the new secular state of India with its eighty-five per cent Hindu majority. Michael Brecher wrote of the movement of refugees:

In sheer numbers it (the cross-migration) was the greatest in history, probably about twelve million, equally divided between

Hindus and Sikhs fleeing from West Punjab and Muslims from (East Punjab). Before the year was out half a million people died, or were murdered.[52]

Gandhi, sadly disillusioned over the failure of non-violence, conducted two fasts 'unto death' in an effort to restore religious toleration. The first of the fasts made a very great impact, and prevented further massacres in Calcutta. Mehta commented that Gandhi,

> broke each of his fasts only after receiving pledges from Hindu, Muslim, and Sikh leaders that they would try to make their people live with each other amicably. The pledges had a miraculous short-term effect, but in the end they did not stem the growing violence.[53]

The events of 1946 and 1947 had led Gandhi to admit that his long experiment in non-violence had ended in failure. The people of India had supported him as a political leader who could exert appropriate pressure on the occupying power and lead them towards independence; but they had not accepted his own view of non-violence as an integral part of a moral and truthful life. Gandhi wrote in 1946:

> I find myself in the midst of exaggeration and falsity. I am unable to discover the truth. There is terrible mutual distrust. Oldest friendships have snapped. Truth and *ahimsa* by which I swear, and which to my knowledge have sustained me for sixty years, seem to fail to show the attributes I have ascribed to them.[54]

And eight months later he wrote:

> I have admitted my mistake. . . . I thought our struggle was based on non-violence, whereas in reality it was no more than passive resistance which essentially is a weapon of the weak. It leads naturally to armed resistance whenever possible.[55]

The communal violence which accompanied partition provided a sad backdrop to the last years of Gandhi's life. The tragedy of that time was summed up by India's new Prime Minister, Jawaharlal Nehru, in a speech in Delhi on 29 September 1947:

> There is in Delhi an old man who has been in every way the father of that nation. This old man has been our guide, philosopher and friend for many a year. On his direction and under

his guidance the nation has marched on to freedom and independence.

What must this old man be thinking now? . . . He must be saying that he had taught the country to fight the entire might of the British with the weapon of non-violence. The struggle had ended and victory had been achieved mainly through non-violence. And now that this old man is at the tail end of his life, we have made him a present of bloodshed and destruction. This is how we have treated the architect of India's freedom.[56]

India had become independent on 15 August 1947, and on 26 January 1948 the new nation became a republic. By that time Gandhi was back in New Delhi, staying in a house owned by Birla, the industrialist. Much of his time was spent with the new leaders of India, who came to him for advice and availed themselves in their own disagreements of the independent judgment of this most unusual politician, who had played a leading role in the nationalist movement but had declined office when power had been achieved.

Characteristically, Gandhi did not only deal with leading politicians. He was regularly visited by ordinary people who came with the traditional Indian desire to have *darshan* of one whom they regarded as a great and holy man. In the late afternoon Gandhi would attend a 'prayer meeting' in the garden of the Birla house. This was a gathering to which crowds of people came, and at which there would be readings from the scriptures of several religions as well as prayer.

On 30 January Gandhi walked from the house towards the meeting place, supporting himself, as he so often did, on the shoulders of two of his young women helpers. About five hundred people had gathered that afternoon, and as Gandhi approached them many ran forward to have his *darshan* and to touch his feet. He detached himself from his two assistants and greeted the people in traditional Indian fashion, hands together in front of his chest. A man stepped forward as if to touch or greet him. But instead of raising his hands in greeting the man lifted a small pistol and fired three shots at Gandhi from point-blank range. Gandhi fell to the ground, his last words the familiar Hindu invocation of God, 'Ram, Ram'.

Gandhi's assassin was a Maharashtrian Brahmin named Nathuram Vinayak Godse. He was captured at the prayer meeting, and Gandhi's disciples retained enough of their principles of non-violence to prevent the crowd from lynching him. Godse was a member of an extreme right-wing Hindu group, the Hindu Mahasabha, who wished to see Hinduism clearly established as the religion of the new nation and preserved from the threats to traditional caste practices which they saw in Gandhi's campaigns for the uplift of the untouchables. Gandhi's attempts at reconciliation between Hindu and Muslim communities were also seen as a threat to the pre-eminence of Hindu religion and culture. During his trial, which lasted nine months, Godse said that he regarded Gandhi's teachings on *ahimsa* as both misguided and dangerous. Godse himself interpreted the *Bhagavad Gita* very differently from Gandhi, and saw it as religious authority for taking up arms against the enemies of Hindu *dharma*. He said:

> I firmly believe that the teachings of absolute *ahimsa* as advocated by Gandhiji would ultimately result in the emasculation of the Hindu community and thus make the community incapable of resisting the aggression or inroads of other communities, especially the Muslims. . .[57]

During the celebrations of the centenary of Gandhi's birth, in 1969, a close relative of Godse wrote an article in *The Hindu* newspaper claiming that events in the twenty-two years since independence had shown Godse to be right.

The majority opinion in India was very different, however. Godse was found guilty of the murder of Gandhi, and although Gandhians appealed for clemency for the assassin, he, together with an accomplice, was hanged on 15 November 1949. In an emotional speech delivered over All India Radio on the night of the assassination, Prime Minister Nehru found words to express the sentiments of many people when he said: 'The light has gone out in our land, and there is darkness everywhere.'[58]

7

The Gandhian Technique of Non-Violence

Gandhi's whole life witnessed to his belief in the significance and power of non-violence. But non-violence as he understood and practised it was not a simple straightforward thing; it was neither the absolute pacifism of the European Quaker nor the world-denying negation of the Indian Jaina. *Satyagraha* had grown out of the meeting of many ideas. Gandhi's belief that renunciation is a central theme of religion was part of *satyagraha*. Jaina and Buddhist *ahimsa* expressed renunciation in practical and well-tried ways. Hinduism had adopted the notion that renunciation is a vital part of religious life. In the *Bhagavad Gita* Gandhi had discovered the idea of *nishkama karma*, a ideal of disinterested service which emphasizes the importance of renunciation.

Gandhi had found renunciation elsewhere, and regarded it as fundamental to other religious traditions. The Sermon on the Mount seemed to him to glow with this theme. 'If any one strikes you on the right cheek, turn to him the other also' struck Gandhi as the epitome of renunciation in practice. The example of Jesus in suffering the crucifixion led Christians to formulate doctrines of the atonement, but seemed to Gandhi chiefly to enact the ideal of renunciation.

His reading of Ruskin's *Unto This Last* had a profound effect on Gandhi's understanding of social theory, and led him to his vigorous campaign against untouchability. Here, too, was renunciation for the caste Hindu. For all to share in the most menial tasks of the community required a shift of values and a renunciation of established custom.

Another influence upon Gandhi during the formative period of his thought was Tolstoy. Leo Tolstoy was fiercely critical of the examples of Christianity provided by the main churches of the

West, and especially of the way in which the Russian Orthodox Church represented Christian values in the Russia of his day. This he regarded as a 'false Christianity, represented by the church, whose principles often differ from those of paganism only by lack of sincerity'.[1]

Tolstoy arrived at a doctrine of absolute pacifism, a 'law of love without exceptions', which he considered to be the only valid interpretation of true Christian doctrine,[2] to be applied to the conduct of nations as rigorously as to the behaviour of individuals. Gandhi, inspired by Tolstoy's ideals, corresponded with the Russian writer during the struggle for civil rights in the Transvaal in 1909. Tolstoy commended the Indians in South Africa in the 'same struggle of the tender against the harsh, of weakness and love against pride and violence. . .'[3] The following April Gandhi again wrote to Tolstoy, sending him a copy of his own book, *Indian Home Rule*.

Gandhi was impressed by Tolstoy. The Russian's Christian pacifism helped Gandhi to clarify the basis of his own non-violence. But Gandhi did not entirely accept the thoroughgoing pacifism of Tolstoy. He responded to Tolstoy as he did to other influences, absorbing ideas, accepting inspiration, but then fitting the inspiration and ideas into his own framework.

For Gandhi the framework was *satyagraha*, and it is important to recognize that *satyagraha* is not pacifism. Of course, it was influenced by the *ahimsa* of Jainism and Buddhism and of Gandhi's native Gujarat; it was influenced by the ideal of the Sermon on the Mount, as Gandhi understood that part of the New Testament; it was influenced by Ruskin and Thoreau and Tolstoy; it was influenced by the idea of disinterested service found in the *nishkama karma* of the *Gita*. But *satyagraha* was nevertheless Gandhi's own concept. He adopted the word *satyagraha* in order to avoid 'pacifism', which he regarded as a negative term describing a negative response to oppression.[4] And although he often used the word *ahimsa* (non-force, or non-violence) to describe his ideal approach to situations of conflict, the positive phrase *satyagraha* remained his normal word for his programme of non-violent civil disobedience. *Satyagraha* is often translated 'non-violence', but of course it does not mean that. The accurate rendering of 'the struggle of truth' does not have about it the ring of a popular slogan, but it does express the positive emphasis which Gandhi was so keen to preserve, and it avoids the doctrinaire position of absolute pacifism.

For most of his life Gandhi held the view that violence could be used in certain circumstances, and that a defensive war is sometimes justified. That was reflected in his participation in the Boer War and the Zulu Rebellion, and his encouragement of the enlistment of medical orderlies in the Great War. In 1920 he wrote:

I do believe that, where there is only a choice between coward- ice and violence, I would advise violence. Thus when my eldest son asked me what he should have done had he been present when I was almost fatally assaulted in 1908, whether he should have run away and seen me killed or whether he should have used his physical force, which he could and wanted to use, and defended me, I told him that it was his duty to defend me even by using violence. Hence it was that I took part in the Boer War, the so-called Zulu Rebellion and the late War. Hence also do I advocate training in arms for those who believe in the method of violence. I would rather have India resort to arms in order to defend her honour than that she would, in a cowardly manner, become or remain a helpless witness to her own dishonour.[5]

In 1921 Gandhi was asked through the columns of *Young India* whether he thought it right that Indian men and money should be used to fight the battles of Britain. His reply was yes, if India had entered into treaty obligations with other nations.[6]

His willingness to encourage Indians to enlist in South Africa and during the First World War was based upon a belief in the British Empire as the defender of justice for all her subjects. If Indians in South Africa were to appeal to London for help in their struggles for justice against the prejudices of local rulers, then, Gandhi thought, they should be prepared to fight for the Empire in a time of need.[7]

However, in a somewhat contradictory fashion, he expressed reservations about the rightness of following the profession of a soldier.

I refuse to call the profession of the sepoy honourable when he has no choice as to the time when and the persons against whom he is called upon to use his sword. The sepoy's services have more often been utilized for enslaving us than for protecting us. . . What will happen during Swaraj is easily answered. The soldiers will form the national militia for defensive and protec- tive purposes alone.[8]

The expectation that in a free nation soldiers could exercise responsible choice about what battles they should fight, or that the causes of an independent nation must necessarily be just, strike the modern observer as remarkably naive.

During the years of the 1920s and 1930s, as Gandhi engaged in non-violent resistance and civil disobedience, his faith in *ahimsa* seems to have grown stronger. By the time of the Second World War he was personally opposed to the use of military force even for national defence, although he conceded that national policy was not likely to follow his idealistic view.[9] But he agreed with the need for an armed police force in an independent India:

> I have to concede that even in a non-violent state a police force may be necessary. This, I admit, is a sign of my imperfect *ahimsa*. I have not the courage to declare that we can carry on without a police force as I have in respect of an army. Of course I can and do envisage a State where the police will not be necessary, but whether we shall succeed in realizing it, the future alone will show. The police of my conception will, however, be of a wholly different pattern from the present day force. Its ranks will be composed of believers in non-violence. They will be servants, not masters, of the people. The people will instinctively render them every help, and through mutual co-operation they will easily deal with the ever decreasing disturbances. The police force will have some kind of arms, but they will be rarely used, if at all. In fact, the policemen will be reformers. Their police work will be confined primarily to robbers and dacoits. Quarrels between labour and capital and strikes will be few and far between in a non-violent State. . .[10]

Here we see the conflict and contradictions in Gandhi's beliefs about non-violence. He looked to an ideal society in a future in which armies would have become obsolete, and police forces could operate gently and kindly in a non-violent society. The robbers and dacoits alone would cloud this scene of mutual helpfulness, and Gandhi conceded that the police would have to deal firmly with them. Earlier in his career, as we have seen, Gandhi acknowledged the need for armed forces, conceded the justice of some military actions, and encouraged his supporters to enlist. The shift in his thinking towards the end of his life seems to me to reflect two things. One is the tendency for ideals to become absolute when there is no immediate prospect of their being adopted. The transformation of ideals into practice involves pragmatic choices and usually an element of compromise. This we see reflected throughout the civil disobedience campaigns in which Gandhi was involved. The issues of the Second World War, however, were far removed from Gandhi's immediate sphere of influence. Realistic choices about a European war could not be made in India. Gandhian techniques could not be applied to that conflict by any existing Gandhians. So an idealized approach did not lead to practical problems. But Gandhi was also an astute politician. His earlier view, that support for the British Empire would strengthen the institution which could guarantee justice for Indian people, had been tempered by circumstances. By 1940 he saw that the appropriate political response for Indian nationalists was opposition to the Empire, and so he had a second reason for opposing involvement in the current military conflict.

This is not to be cynical about Gandhi's genuine belief in the essential rightness of non-violence. But it is to recognize that he was not consistently devoted to a thoroughgoing *ahimsa* on the Jaina pattern, nor was he an absolute pacifist.

For Gandhi, non-violence was a technique which preserved the truth and expressed goodness in situations of human conflict, but it was not a dogma to be applied indiscriminately in every situation.

For example, Gandhi did not entirely share the conviction, implicit in absolute *ahimsa*, that the killing of animals is wrong. In 1946 he wrote:

> I have no feeling in me to save the life of those animals which devour or cause hurt to man. . . I have come to the conclusion that to do away with monkeys where they have become a menace to the well-being of man is pardonable. Such killing becomes a duty.[11]

The refusal to be bound by a dogmatic interpretation of *ahimsa* is also reflected in Gandhi's approach to situations of human conflict. At a seminar on the Gandhian concept of non-violence in 1971 Stuart Nelson accurately summarized this point:

> In relation to non-violence Mahatma Gandhi was not an absolutist. The perfection which Gandhi taught was the perfection of striving and not of attainment, for he believed perfection to be unattainable. He saw perfect non-violence as impossible as long as we are in a physical state. . . This eloquent and unwearying preacher of non-violence conceded that there were occasions which justified its abandonment. There are times, he said, when the taking of a life becomes a duty, as when we destroy life to sustain the body, or in the interests in health we

kill the mosquito or other disease carrier. To dispatch the lunatic who runs amuck killing everyone in his path, when there is no possibility of capturing him alive, is to earn the gratitude of the community . . . Gandhi went further. Though a believer in non-violence, he conceived instances when duty would require him to vote for the military training of those who had no objections to it.[12]

This helps to explain Gandhi's preference for the word *satyagraha*, the struggle of truth. His emphasis was upon positive qualities. The *satyagrahi* was required to demonstrate courage, selflessness, compassion, and a great desire to see justice done. *Satyagraha* is not the passive acquiescence of the weak, but the truly strong standing up for what is right and true.

Because *satyagraha* was seen by Gandhi as the struggle of truth, the relationship between means and ends was regarded as critically important. One could not fight for truth in a deceptive way, nor use unjust means to secure justice. The *satyagrahi* had to use methods which reflected his commitment to truth and justice and peace. Gandhi told his followers that to resort to unjust means in order to defeat the injustices of foreign rule would inevitably result in the continuation of injustice under different leadership. 'If we were to drive out the English with the weapons with which they enslaved us, our slavery would still be with us even when they have gone.'[13] Gandhi impressed upon his followers the belief that *satya*, or truth, must ultimately prevail if pursued by truthful means, and confidence in the eventual victory of the true and just cause was an essential part of the *satyagrahi*'s equipment.

Curiously, although Gandhi's non-violence was in many respects pragmatic rather than dogmatic, in other areas of activity the Mahatma showed a firm attachment to unwavering beliefs in what to the observer appear to be trivialities. Undergirding his philosophy of non-violence was a view of life strongly influenced by his Gujarati background. For example, his belief in the value of absolute chastity to the religious life and his pernickety attachment to vegetarianism reveal the extent and the nature of his Hindu frame of thought.

M. M. Thomas has drawn attention to the way in which Gandhi regarded the physical as grossly inferior to the spiritual.[14] The human body he regarded as alien to the soul, and he conceived of spiritual liberation as being found in the deliverance of the soul from the body.

Within such a framework of theological thought, there is an

ultimately negative attitude to the human body which is seen at best as a necessary evil to be put up with and used for the time being. It is this approach to the body and its relation to the essential soul that leads Gandhi to equate body-force with violence and soul-force with non-violence.[15]

It is within this context that Gandhi regarded sex and marriage, material prosperity, taking pleasure in food and drink and dress, and the use of body-force to gain political ends as undesirable. They all belonged to the area of *himsa* and body-force which he saw as directly opposed to soul-force and *ahimsa*. Mahatma Gandhi made asceticism an essential part of his non-violence and in so doing limited the appeal of his *satyagraha*. Thomas wisely commented:

> Gandhi's was an *ahimsa* transformed by the influence of *agape*; but the ascetic attitudes of *ahimsa* followed it throughout, and sometimes even dominated it. This was most evident in his attitude to sex and power-politics, which have made Sarvodaya dogmatic and largely irrelevant to a nation committed to modernity in its political, economic and social development.[16]

In this respect Gandhi was very different from his Western admirer, Martin Luther King Jr, who applied Gandhian techniques of non-violence without accepting the ascetic tradition which was so important to Gandhi.

Gandhi, then was an absolutist in some areas of behaviour. He had very doctrinaire attitudes towards vegetarianism, celibacy, birth-control, and nature cures, but the central doctrine of *ahimsa*, which infused *satyagraha*, he acknowledged as an ethic whose method of application would vary with each situation.

Satyagraha was for him a technique, involving a ruthless regard for honesty, a fearless desire to right wrong, and an attempt to understand an opponent's point of view. He frequently contrasted 'the non-violence of the weak' with 'the non-violence of the strong', believing *satyagraha* to be a weapon which could be employed effectively only by those who were trained and courageous.[17] This he constantly stressed, and when, in the critical months of 1946 and 1947, the values of *ahimsa* and *satyagraha* as Gandhi had preached them appeared to have been rejected, he was bitterly disappointed. The entire set of values, including *ahimsa*, which had inspired Gandhi's political and religious life, and which he had displayed, sometimes theatrically, on every possible occasion, had won him an invincible position for many years as the greatest all-India political leader. But when Independence came, Gandhi, still idolized by many, found his ideals rejected.

Nevertheless, his passionate belief in *satyagraha* inspired others to adapt this part of his teaching to their own local situations. The best-known example of this is Martin Luther King Jr, who deliberately borrowed from India the system of non-violent protest which Gandhi had constructed by grafting Western ideas on to the ancient doctrine of *ahimsa*.[18]

This adaptation of Gandhian methods to places outside India and times other than Gandhi's own suggests that *satyagraha* can be isolated from the total package of Gandhian philosophy. Vegetarianism, cow-protection, home-spinning, Hindi language, a campaign against untouchability, and an ostentatiously simple style of living were all part of the Gandhi image. But it is possible to isolate *satyagraha* from these other concerns, identify its characteristics, and assess its more general value.[19]

Mahatma Gandhi had assumed that *satyagraha* was a natural expression of *ahimsa*, that *ahimsa* was deeply rooted in the Indian character, and that therefore it would gain widespread acceptance in India. Events in 1946/47 showed the weakness of this assumption. In spite of the gentle character of many Indian people, mob violence was no less possible in India than elsewhere. The terrible events at the time of partition, with the deaths of millions of Hindus and Muslims in communal violence, was seen by Gandhi as a terrible defeat for his most cherished ideas. And with her independence secure, India paid lip-service to Gandhi but rejected most of his specific teaching. Gandhiji appears to have shared the fate of some other great moral and religious leaders: the adulation accorded to him is often in inverse proportion to the admirer's willingness actually to embrace his teaching.

The failure of *satyagraha* after Gandhi seems to me to have been partially due to a lack of appreciation of the differences between traditional *ahimsa* and Gandhian *satyagraha*. Because *satyagraha* was the result of a mixing of ideas from different sources, many of his followers failed to understand or enter into Gandhi's idea of *satyagraha*; this contributed to the ambivalent attitudes of his fellow freedom fighters, and contributed to the failure of *satyagraha* after Independence.

Satyagraha as Gandhi taught it was not simply *ahimsa* applied to the twentieth century, although it owed much to *ahimsa*. Gandhi borrowed freely and dispassionately from many sources. As a Hindu, speaking chiefly to Hindus, it was natural for him to

identify non-violence with *ahimsa* and to press Hindu authorities
to the support of his system. But his own spiritual and political
pilgrimage was highly unusual, and brought together a wide range
of ideas.

For Gandhi, non-violence, unlike most of the causes he es-
poused, was not a dogma. He was prepared to admit compromise.
It was not so much an unshakable belief as a technique, to be
applied differently to different situations. The technique has been
defined well by Joan Bondurant:

> Non-violence when used in connection with Satyagraha means
> the exercise of power or influence to effect change without
> injury to the opponent.[20]

This technique has some roots in *ahimsa*. But *ahimsa* alone,
with its firm ideas of renunciation and its largely negative emphasis, cannot supply all that is demanded by *satyagraha*. For it is a
technique of love. To be fully effective it must include, as Gandhi
often urged, the desire to do good even to one's opponent. It is
not likely to succeed, as Gandhi's theory did not explicitly
acknowledge, when used without passion and without a deep
concern for human relationships.

For, largely unnoticed, there slipped into the technique of
non-violence and *satyagraha* a strong flavour of the New Testament. It included things gleaned by Gandhiji from his reading of
the Sermon on the Mount. It was summarized in such vivid illustrations of the ethic of Christ as, 'Love your enemies and pray for
your persecutors', and in the Pauline injunctions: 'Bless those
who persecute you', and 'Do not be overcome with evil, but
overcome evil with good.'[21]

The technique of non-violence is helped by the New Testament
understanding that love, expressed in practical human relationships, is what chiefly contributes to the knowledge of God, and
that such love is itself a reflection of a God of grace and forgiveness.[22] It is significant that in practice this aspect of the New
Testament had been largely ignored by Christians for centuries,
until Gandhi brought it into political use.

So it is no surprise that Gandhi's *satyagraha* has aroused widespread interest and admiration throughout the world in a way that
his other ideas have not. The interest is not confined to the
political aspects of his campaigns, but includes a genuine desire
to know how high ethical principles can be applied to the hard
realities of social relationships.

For in spite of his failures, Mahatma Gandhi gave the world an unparalleled demonstration of a technique for loving; a technique which resolutely seeks justice, but also desires only good for those against whom the struggle is carried out; a technique which demands of its users much courage, tenacity, and sensitivity; and a technique which blends in an unusually effective way moral and spiritual insights from East and West.

8

Martin Luther King Jr

In Gandhi's thought and technique there was a blending of East and West. I have suggested that one part of the failure of India fully to understand and apply Gandhianism was due to a lack of knowledge of the nature of Christian love as described in the New Testament and exemplified in the life of Jesus. But the record of the West shows no greater depth of understanding of the practice of self-sacrificing love. During the first few centuries of the church's life, as we have seen, Christians appear to have regarded pacifism as the proper response to the claims of armies and warfare, although they were not successful in reconciling their ideal of love with the demands made upon them by the exercise of temporal power after the conversion of Constantine.[1] Ways were found of imposing theoretical limits upon the nature of warfare in which Christians might legitimately engage; the theory of the just war was constructed. But different rules were applied to warfare against infidels and heretics, and some of the worst excesses of war were perpetrated in battles which were intended to defend the faith. The early church's attitude of Christian pacifism was adhered to only by small minorities among Christians, for whom it was an absolute demand of a law of love, regardless of the difficulty of accommodating pacifism to the needs of the state.

There is a certain irony in the fact that the inspiration provided by Gandhi is leading to a reinterpretation of the technique of non-violent resistance in the West. The meeting of ideas from various religious traditions has already contributed to fresh insight into the nature of pacifism and non-violent resistance. The most notable example of the use of Gandhian techniques in the West is that of Martin Luther King Jr in the civil rights movement in the USA during the 1950s and 1960s.

Martin Luther King Jr deliberately adopted Gandhian techniques, regarded them as particularly appropriate to the struggle for civil rights for blacks in the United States, and was committed to a philosophy of non-violence which in many respects was remarkably similar to that of Mahatma Gandhi. Many of those who now admire Martin Luther King regard his non-violence as a modern example of Christian pacifism.[2] In this I believe they are mistaken, and certainly such an understanding fails to do justice to Gandhianism. But Gandhianism itself seems to be little understood by many of those who today seek to carry further the work of Martin Luther King Jr. Yet to understand the positive contribution of Martin King and his civil rights workers to the practice of non-violent resistance it is vital that the distinctions between doctrinaire pacifism and Gandhianism be appreciated.

Martin Luther King Jr grew up in Georgia, when blacks in the southern states of the USA were subject to many disabilities and indignities. But his own early life was cushioned from the harshness which was part of the experience of many blacks. He was born on 15 January 1929 at a house on Auburn Avenue, Atlanta, near to the Baptist church of which his father was minister.[3] It was a time when considerable status and influence accrued to ministers of black churches in the United States, and the King family were respected and leading members of the important black community of Atlanta. So although potentially subject to the disabilities imposed upon blacks by society, Martin King spent his childhood in a relatively privileged environment.

He was a bright child, and progressed rapidly through school. In September 1944, well before his sixteenth birthday, he entered Morehouse College in Atlanta to begin a degree course. He had passed the college entrance examination without first graduating from high school.[4] By June 1948 he had gained a BA degree, with sociology as the major subject. Perhaps even more important than this indication of early academic ability was his decision, taken during his time at Morehouse, to follow in his father's footsteps and become a minister. Baptists, of course, upheld the right of independent churches to ordain their own ministers, and on 25 February 1948, at the astonishingly early age of nineteen, Martin Luther King Jr was ordained in Ebenezer Baptist Church, Atlanta. At that point he could have become co-pastor of Ebenezer, his father's church, and developed what promised to be a great reputation as a rousing preacher in a comfortable Atlanta environment, where the black community prized the gifts of the emotionally stimulating preacher more highly than almost any other abilities.

But before embarking upon a lifetime's ministry, Martin King wanted to enlarge his theological education. His father was persuaded to allow him to proceed to Crozer Theological Seminary, at Chester in Pennsylvania. Whilst a student at Morehouse, Martin had lived at home; in choosing to enrol at Crozer he elected to spend time in a different environment, and this probably gave him an opportunity to mature, as well as providing a wider view of society than was contained within his home community in Atlanta. It also gave him the opportunity to read more widely and to mature as a student. It was while he was at Crozer that Martin's interest in Mahatma Gandhi was first aroused. He attended a talk given by Dr Mordecai Johnson, President of Howard University, on a recent visit to India, including some enthusiastic comments about Gandhi. Martin was extremely impressed:

> His message was so profound and electrifying that I left the meeting and bought a half-dozen books on Gandhi's life and works.[5]

At Crozer, Martin King read Niebuhr, and was challenged by Niebuhr's rejection of pacifism. He concluded that Niebuhr misunderstood 'true pacifism' which, Martin King claimed, 'is not unrealistic submission to evil power. . . It is rather a courageous confrontation of evil by the power of love . . .'[6] But other aspects of Niebuhr's writings, especially his emphasis on pragmatism in assessing the value of a social gospel, appealed greatly to Martin.

He also read Nietzsche, and devoted his Christmas vacation in 1949 to a study of Marx. In later life it is clear that Martin Luther King was firmly opposed to communism; as a student he was repelled by the atheistic and deterministic aspects of Marxian thought; yet he recognized in his reading of Marx a compensation for the church's failures to apply its message to economic and social issues. Some observers have thought of King as economically a Marxist.[7]

In June 1951 Martin Luther King graduated from Crozer with a BD degree. But his three years of further study had convinced him that he wanted to pursue academic work further. He had graduated at Crozer with the best grades in his class. In addition to that confirmation of his ability, his enquiring mind had identified areas of study he wished to pursue further. It seemed logical to go on and attempt a doctorate. In September 1951 he enrolled at Boston University to work towards a PhD in theology. His dissertation was on 'A Comparison of the Conceptions of God in the Thinking of Paul Tillich and Henry Nelson Wieman'. Both the thinkers he studied had adopted a somewhat impersonalistic view of God. Against that, Martin King argued for a more personalistic view. It seemed to him, practically as well as intellectually, that if religion were to be real and relevant to matters of everyday life, then it had to be fed by belief in a personal God who is himself concerned with personal affairs and with social justice.

In an important biography of Martin Luther King, David L. Lewis suggests that the civil rights leader was not a person of especially high intellectual ability. He describes him as:

> Essentially a Baptist preacher whose extraordinary rhetorical abilities were not quite matched by practical intelligence and political radicalism.[8]

And of his doctoral work, Lewis writes:

> A candid assessment of his abilities must hold that, despite his broad reading and rigorous application, Mike lacked the comprehensive critical apparatus and the inspired vision that bless good philosophers. Although he was of a tolerant cast of mind, his intellectual range was, in fact, narrow.[9]

This view, however, is contested by Dr Harold DeWolf, who supervised Martin Luther King's doctoral studies at Boston University, and remained a close confidant for the rest of King's life. In a personal conversation, Dr DeWolf told me that Martin King was an exceptional PhD student.[10] One example of the speed, accuracy, and application of his work was that he was required to support his PhD programme with a reading knowledge of Greek and German. Experience with most students showed that it normally took a year to reach the required standard in languages. Martin King, knowing of the requirement, had begun to study before he went to Boston, and asked for a test almost as soon as he arrived. He took the test and passed.

During thirty-one years at Boston University Dr DeWolf had forty PhD students, and he ranked Martin Luther King among the best two or three. He was sure that Martin King would have made an excellent academic had it been possible for him to pursue such a career.

On this assessment, by somebody who knew Dr King extraordinarily well and was especially well-placed to judge his intellectual ability, there seems to be little doubt of his high level of 'practical intelligence'. So far as his 'intellectual range' is concerned, circumstances forced King into the concerns of the civil rights movement. Had he lived beyond his short life of thirty-nine years it seems likely that he would eventually have given himself to reflective thought and intellectual pursuits, and there seems to be no reason to doubt his ability to succeed in this.

In June 1953 Martin married Coretta Scott, who had been a student at the New England Conservatory of Music. The following year the young Dr King accepted an appointment as Pastor of Dexter Avenue Baptist Church in Montgomery, Alabama. So far as he had a plan in his mind for his future career, it would seem that he expected eventually to use his theological studies to the full and engage in teaching, perhaps in a seminary.[11] But first he thought it wise to obtain experience of pastoral work so that he would know at first-hand the work for which he might later prepare students. Circumstances decreed otherwise. Events in Montgomery were to shape his future in a remarkable way.

On 1 December 1955, a Negro woman, Rosa Parks, refused to give up her seat in a Montgomery bus to a white passenger. She had just finished a hard day's work and she was tired. But the law enforced segregation on buses. Whites sat at one end and blacks at the other. The middle section could be used by blacks, but only so long as no white person wanted to sit there. As the bus Rosa Parks travelled on filled up, white passengers began to stand. The driver asked the blacks in the middle section to move to the back and stand. Some did so, but for some reason she could not explain – except to say that she was tired – Rosa Parks stayed where she was and refused to be moved. A policeman was called and she was arrested.

So began the Montgomery bus boycott which launched Martin Luther King Jr on his career as a civil rights leader.

Segregation was commonplace in the South, of course. Blacks and whites were educated separately, ate separately, and travelled separately. The blacks were effectively second-class citizens, with most of them not even registered to vote. Yet there was a growing sense of unease and impatience that discrimination continued year after year in spite of many attempts to change the situation.

The Montgomery bus-boycott was by no means the beginning of civil rights protests in the United States. Campaigns had been waged before, and for many years there had been protests, marches, and integrated bus-rides aimed at relaxing segregation. For example, in 1947 there occurred the Journey of Reconciliation, a freedom ride into the South which grew out of the Irene

Morgan case.[12] Irene Morgan was a black woman who got on a bus in Baltimore, Maryland, to travel south. When the bus reached the Potomac and was crossing into Virginia the driver told Irene Morgan to move to another place on the bus. In the South the buses were segregated. Out of that incident there arose a case before the Supreme Court, based on the plea that segregation was an undue burden on the commerce of inter-state travel. The Supreme Court held that it was. The following year a group of civil rights activists, blacks and whites together, travelled the buses from Washington to Virginia, North Carolina, and Tennessee in order to test the Supreme Court decision. To the six or seven people who spent two weeks together on that journey, the Gandhian ideas and examples of non-violence were important. There was nothing original in the situations or tactics of the Montgomery bus-boycott in 1955. What was unusual was the attention and support it attracted.

The moment for blacks to resist discrimination appears to have come in December 1955, and by the accidents of history and of the personalities involved, the events in Montgomery began to attract widespread attention. The community rallied around Mrs Parks in a remarkable way. There were a number of leaders who felt that her case provided the ideal opportunity to express the growing determination of blacks to challenge the discrimination from which they suffered. The early initiatives were taken by E. D. Nixon, of the National Association of Colored People, and Jo Ann Robinson, of the Women's Political Council. Mrs Robinson drafted a notice to the black people of Montgomery which read:

Don't ride the bus to work, to town, to school, or any place Monday, December 5. Another Negro woman has been arrested and put in jail because she refused to give up her bus seat.

Don't ride the bus to work, to town, to school, or anywhere on Monday. If you work, take a cab, or share a ride, or walk.

Come to a mass meeting, Monday at 7.00 p.m., at the Holt Street Baptist Church for further instruction.[13]

The response was immediate and almost complete. On 5 December, the day of Mrs Parks' trial, less than a dozen black people used the buses.

Rosa Parks' pastor in Montgomery was the Revd Ralph Abernathy, of the First Baptist Church, later to become a well-known leader of the civil rights movement in the States. He had readily agreed to co-operate with E. D. Nixon in plans to organize the boycott. Nixon telephoned Martin King to ask for his assistance and co-operation. After some reflection (his first reaction had been to say: 'Brother Nixon, let me think it out for a while. Call me back'),[14] Martin Luther King agreed to join them. The fact that he soon became the best-known of the Montgomery black leaders was due in part to the coincidence of circumstances. The likeliest leader was E. D. Nixon, who was an official of the Brotherhood of Sleeping Car Porters, but whose work on the trains took him away from Montgomery before the boycott could begin. Lewis comments:

> Had he (Nixon) been able to serve, it is highly unlikely that Martin's talents would have been fully utilized.[15]

Rosa Parks had sparked off the revolt, but the blacks of Montgomery were determined not to let it finish with her trial (she was fined $10, and an appeal against her conviction was lodged). Ralph Abernathy suggested the formation of a Montgomery Improvement Association. A president was needed. Lewis suggests that the community recognized the need for a leader who could be 'a dynamic speaker, with intelligence and character', but that he should also be someone who had not resided long enough in Montgomery to have formed enemies among the disputatious black community, have the prospect of alternative employment elsewhere, be free from the fear of economic retribution from the white community, and 'be sufficiently naive or brave to accept designation as the exclusive leader of the boycott'.[16]

Martin Luther King Jr was elected. He had to address a mass meeting as the new President at very short notice. And on that first occasion he revealed the talent for rousing oratory which was to become so important a part of his appeal. In his speech that night the colourful phrases and the heaped metaphors rang out:

> . . . there comes a time when people get tired of being trampled over by the iron feet of oppression. There comes a time, my friends, when people get tired of being flung across the abyss of humiliation. . . We are here this evening because we are tired now. Now let us say that we are not advocating violence. We have overcome that. I want it to be known throughout Montgomery and throughout this nation that we are a Christian people. We believe in the teaching of Jesus. The only weapon we have in our hands this evening is the weapon of protest . . . don't let anybody make us feel that we ought to be compared in our actions with the Ku Klux Klan or with the White

Citizen's Council. There will be no crosses burned at any bus stops in Montgomery. There will be no white persons pulled out of their homes and taken out on some distant road and murdered. There will be nobody among us who will stand up and defy the Constitution of this nation. We only assemble here because of our desire to see right exist.[17]

The oratory that would appeal to a black Christian gathering was there even in that hastily prepared speech. But so too was the expression of a determination to base the protest on a recognizable Christian ethic.

The boycott was a remarkable success. The black community organized itself with great efficiency. A car pool was established and maintained over a period of twelve months. Prosperous blacks who did not have to depend on buses were drawn into the boycott by the use of their cars and their services as drivers for poorer members of the community.

Inevitably, there was reaction from some members of the white community, who resented the spirited resistance of blacks to discrimination. On 30 January 1956 Martin Luther King's house was dynamited. His family was unharmed, but even so it was a testimony to his deeply-held convictions that, standing on the porch of his damaged home, Martin King could say:

We believe in law and order. Don't get panicky. Don't do anything at all. Don't get out your weapons. He who lives by the sword will perish by the sword. Remember, that is what God said. We are not advocating violence. We want to love our enemies. We must love our white brothers no matter what they do to us.[18]

The commitment to a non-violent technique of protest which came to be associated with Martin King, and which he sometimes had to defend against the strictures of other black leaders, was already present in the early days of the Montgomery boycott. Later, Dr King wrote:

From the beginning a basic philosophy guided the movement. This guiding principle has since been referred to variously as non-violent resistance, non-co-operation, and passive resistance. But in the first days of the protest none of these expressions was mentioned; the phrase most often heard was 'Christian love'. It was the Sermon on the Mount, rather than a doctrine of passive resistance, that initially inspired the Negroes of Montgomery to dignified social action. It was Jesus of

Nazareth that stirred the Negroes to protest with the creative weapon of love. . . As the days unfolded, however, the inspiration of Mahatma Gandhi began to exert its influence.[19]

Parallels with other conflicts, and especially with other non-violent movements and philosophies, were also being drawn by other people. The *Montgomery Advertiser* published a letter which said:

Not since the first battle of the Marne has the taxi been put to as good use as it has this last week in Montgomery. However, the spirit animating our Negro citizens as they ride these taxis or walk from the heart of Cloverdale to Mobile Road has been more like that of Gandhi than of any 'taxicab army' that saved Paris.[20]

At the end of February Bayard Rustin and Glenn Smiley (the field secretary of the Fellowship of Reconciliation) arrived in Montgomery. Lewis, who considered the pacifist influence on the civil rights movement to be silly and demeaning, suggests that,

there is more than coincidence, certainly, in the fact that, from this point on, Martin began to lace his discourses with Gandhian terminology.[21]

The FOR workers helped in a programme of mass education in the tactics of non-violent resistance, whilst the organization provided money and equipment to produce a film on non-violent techniques. They also gave lectures and demonstrations related to the methods of non-violence. The FOR material drew upon Gandhi's work in India to a considerable extent. Clearly, one of the major problems of non-violent resistance conducted over a long period is the maintenance of discipline and morale in order to prevent frustrated supporters from giving vent to violent feelings. This was something Gandhi had often succeeded in doing during the 1920s and 1930s, although his failures to do so have also been noted. It must be said that the Montgomery bus boycott achieved a very high level of success in keeping a whole community disciplined and on the whole non-violent.

In May 1956 a panel of judges declared the Montgomery bus ordinance (relating to the segregation of blacks and whites) unconstitutional. An appeal was lodged, and the white community continued to try to undermine the boycott, turning their attention to ways in which they might destroy the operation of the car pool. In November an appeal was made to the courts for an injunction declaring the car pool a public nuisance and an unlicensed private enterprise. The injunction was granted, but at the same time the Supreme Court declared Alabama's state and local laws requiring segregation on buses unconstitutional. Another month was to pass before the federal order was received and implemented in Montgomery. But early on the morning of 21 December 1956, Martin Luther King Jr, Ralph Abernathy, Ed Nixon and Glenn Smiley boarded a Montgomery bus for a symbolic desegregated ride.[22] A momentous battle had been won by the weapons of non-violence and by the determination of the community.

Through the Montgomery boycott Martin King had worked out and tested a method of social and political protest which expressed his convictions about how the ideals of the Sermon on the Mount could be translated into effective action. He was now well known. In February 1957 *Time Magazine* carried the twenty-eight-year-old preacher's photograph on its cover, and so accorded him one of the notable accolades of the American media. He was already trapped – at the time probably quite willingly – in the public image that was to hold him until his death.

In January 1957 the Southern Leadership Conference was founded in a meeting at Ebenezer Baptist Church in Atlanta, and Martin Luther King Jr was elected President. Originally termed the Southern Leadership Conference on Transportation and Non-Violent Integration, it was intended to provide an organization to build on the achievements of Montgomery. A month later, in New Orleans, the organization changed its name to the Southern Negro Leadership Conference. This in turn was to become the Southern Christian Leadership Conference, and as such was to become the main organizational instrument of King's policies, the official institutional embodiment of the method of non-violent resistance as the model for effecting social change in the South.[23]

The SCLC has remained active as the leading Christian organization working for the rights of blacks in the Southern States. It was in the forefront of the civil rights campaign in the 1950s and 1960s, and in recent times has turned its attention increasingly to the economic problems of black Americans. As a spokesman of the SCLC said to me in Atlanta in August 1980:

> Now that we can sit at the lunch counters and go to the hotels we don't have the money to pay for it.[24]

This emphasis is a logical development of the concerns that Martin Luther King had towards the end of his life, and rests upon the assumption that basically unemployment, like racism, is a moral issue. The SCLC sees itself as essentially a Christian organization, expressing the authentic voice of the Christian church, and following in a tradition in which the demands of black Americans for justice and equality in American society have been presented as the voice of Christian values appealing to the Christian conscience of the USA. In this it sees itself today as the true inheritor of the mantle of Martin Luther King Jr.

> The SCLC is an arm of the Church. It was conceived in the Church, and was founded by a Baptist preacher. Dr King said first of all he was a preacher. Dr Abernathy who succeeded him was a preacher. . .[25]

Unfortunately for the inheritance of Martin Luther King, there has in recent times been a split between the leadership of the SCLC and the family of Martin King. Dr King's widow, Coretta Scott King, is actively involved in the formation of a 'Martin Luther King Jr Center for Nonviolent Social Change', also located at Auburn Avenue, Atlanta, just a few hundred yards from the headquarters of the SCLC. The objectives of the two organizations appear to be similar, and I suspect that the emergence of the new organization is the result of a difference of opinion about who can properly be regarded as the true successors of Dr King. From a visit to Atlanta and conversations with many people in the civil rights movement, the SCLC, and the King family,[26] I gained the impression that on the one hand there is a desire to preserve the memory of Martin Luther King inviolate and to build a great monument to his life and achievements. So his tomb in Atlanta, the Ebenezer Baptist Church, the Center for Nonviolent Social Change, all seem calculated to become centres of pilgrimage with a reference point in the past. On the other hand, the SCLC seems to me to be chiefly concerned with pursuing in the present and the future the kind of programme which they see developing logically from the moral and spiritual idealism of Southern black Christians; in that they acknowledge their debt to Martin Luther King Jr, but do not seem so tempted to make a mausoleum of his memory.

In September 1957 the first of Martin Luther King's four books, *Stride Toward Freedom: the Montgomery Story*, was published,[27] and with this his reputation as the foremost leader of black Christians in the South was enhanced. The perils of such public attention were illustrated, however, when on 20 September he was stabbed by a woman whilst autographing copies of the book in a bookshop in Harlem. The wound was superficial, and the assailant said to be mentally deranged, but the incident was an ominous sign of the conflicting and sometimes violent emotions which could be aroused by a Christian leader involved in contentious social and political issues.

Martin King's attachment to Gandhian ideals had also become well known, and in 1959 he was invited by Prime Minister Jawaharlal Nehru to visit India and study Gandhianism there. Dr and Mrs King spent from 2 February to 10 March in India, where Dr King met Gandhians, learned more of the work of Gandhi, and was undoubtedly subjected to a certain amount of propaganda which he appears to have accepted at face value. Lewis describes the meeting in New Delhi between Pandit Nehru and Martin Luther King.

> Their talk naturally turned to the alleviation of religious and racial suffering, and Nehru spoke compassionately of his government's determination to eradicate vestiges of caste. Three times during the week, Martin was to read the pronouncements of the Prime Minister on untouchability. He reflected upon the contrast between governmental concern in India with social injustice and the quiescence of federal authority in his own country.[28]

Did Martin King really believe that the prime minister's pronouncements were having a radical effect on caste discrimination? Or that there were only 'vestiges' of caste left in India? If so, it was a naive belief. In spite of official government pronouncements, caste discrimination continues to be a significant and sometimes vicious element in Indian life twenty years after the Kings' visit.

However, Martin appears to have gained much from his visit to India. He visited a number of Gandhian centres, and spoke to many enthusiasts for the work of Gandhi. He learned much more of the actual tactics employed by Gandhi in the civil disobedience movement in India. Lewis considers that the visit had been critical in confirming Martin Luther King's conviction that Gandhian non-violent resistance was the right path for American blacks to tread in their struggle for justice.

> It made the difference between an emotionally based intellectual conviction that non-violence was a morally superior and practical philosophy and certitude founded upon empirical and generalized observation of this philosophy in daily operation.[29]

Of course, he had not seen the Gandhian movement in operation;

only the Gandhian legacy, and the small number of people in India who continued to believe in the teachings and example of the Mahatma long after the nationalist movement and an independent government had abandoned them. Nevertheless, Gandhi's philosophy of non-violence and the example of the Indian *satyagraha* campaigns remained very important to King; how he understood the Indian movement we shall consider later.

At the end of 1959 Martin Luther King announced his intention of resigning from the pastorate of Dexter Avenue Baptist Church in Montgomery. The conflict of duties between a busy city pastorate and the increasing demands made upon him by his leading role in the civil rights movement had become too much. In January 1960 he moved back to Atlanta (where the SCLC headquarters were located) and became co-pastor of his father's church, Ebenezer Baptist. From that base he was free to devote more time to the issues that increasingly demanded his attention.

9

Non-Violence or Black Power?

During his first few months back in Atlanta Martin Luther King worked extremely hard to build up the SCLC. Many others were active in the movement, but it was the inspiration of his personality and leadership that provided the main impetus for the growth of the organization. In addition to his undoubted intellectual gifts and his power as an orator, Martin King was a very hard worker and extremely efficient in his use of time. It was not unusual for him to work eighteen hours a day, and to cram into those hours a great many activities – planning, organizing, preaching, speaking, touring the country, and increasingly establishing himself as one of the most potent voices of black America.

But the civil rights movement was not a one-man concern; many others were involved in their own forms of protest against the disabilities suffered by blacks in the Southern States. In February 1960, just after Dr King's return to Atlanta, two black students in Greensboro, North Carolina, wanted to eat at the lunch counter at their local bus terminal. They were refused on the grounds that 'we don't serve Negroes'. Joined by two more students, they went next day to Woolworths, and received the same treatment. They decided to begin their own form of non-violent protest. They went each day to the store, the staff refusing to serve them but they sitting silently in protest at the discrimination. The idea caught on among other students, who saw in this activity an immediate and attractive form of protest which initially did not require elaborate organization. The movement spread to other towns in North Carolina, then to Tennessee, and on to Atlanta.

In April, SCLC provided financial support for a civil rights student conference held at Shaw University, Raleigh, North Carolina. The two principal speakers were Martin Luther King and

James Lawson (who had been dismissed from Vanderbilt University for participating in a lunch-counter sit-in at Nashville). The conference led to the eventual formation of the Student Non-violent Coordinating Committee (or SNCC), which, although expressing a separate student identity with some ideas different from those of SCLC, was strongly influenced at its inception by the ideas and personality of Martin Luther King. Speaking at the Raleigh Conference, Dr King emphasised the importance he attached to non-violence:

> Another element in our struggle . . . is reconciliation. Our ultimate end must be the creation of the beloved community. The tactics of nonviolence without the spirit of nonviolence may become a new kind of violence.[1]

He also suggested the formation of a corps of volunteers who would be willing to accept prison sentences instead of paying fines. Here was a direct application of a Gandhian technique. The new student organization incorporated into its statement of purpose a declaration of its intent to be non-violent:

> We affirm the philosophical or religious ideal of nonviolence as the foundation of our purpose, the presupposition of our faith, and the manner of our action. Nonviolence as it grows from the Judaic-Christian tradition seeks a social order of justice permeated by love.[2]

The students who participated in the sit-ins needed great discipline and self-control. They were often abused by white customers or bystanders, and in some places there were vigorous attempts on the part of whites to provoke those taking part in the sit-ins (both blacks and whites) to retaliation. Photographs of jeering white youths pouring ketchup and other culinary delicacies over the heads of the students sitting quietly at the counters indicates how great was the provocation and how strong the self-control of most of the demonstrators.

Many students carried reminders of the ideal of non-violence in printed notices which read:

> Remember the teachings of Jesus Christ, Mahatma Gandhi, and Martin Luther King. Remember love and nonviolence.[3]

The Revd Ed Brown, of Atlanta, who participated in the sit-ins, told me how there were not only volunteers at the counters bearing the indignities and waiting patiently for the service which did not come, but that there were other volunteers whose task was to stay in the background and act as witnesses, so that if demonstrators were taken to court there were witnesses to vouch for their non-violent behaviour.[4]

Martin Luther King was himself arrested in connection with a sit-in. He had gone with a number of other people, mostly students, to Rich's department store in Atlanta and asked to be served at the lunch counter. He was arrested on a charge of trespassing. That particular charge was not proceeded with. But shortly before this, Martin King had been charged with a minor traffic infringement in neighbouring De Kalb county. The sentence for that violation had been a small fine and a suspended twelve-month prison sentence. The charge of trespassing provided the opportunity for Judge Mitchell, in De Kalb county, to declare that Dr King had violated the terms of his probation, and to sentence him immediately to four months hard labour at Reidsville State prison.[5] The imprisonment caused an uproar. From across the country and around the world people protested at the harsh sentence. The matter became a political issue. It was the time of the Presidential campaign between Richard Nixon and John F. Kennedy. Nixon remained silent on the issue, but John Kennedy telephoned Coretta King to express his sympathy and support for her husband, while Robert Kennedy telephoned Judge Mitchell to enquire why Dr King could not be granted bail. Some commentators believe that this had a significant effect on the result of the close-run Presidential contest. Certainly Martin Luther King Sr was impressed. Previously a Republican and supporter of Richard Nixon, he told his congregation:

> It took courage to call my daughter-in-law at a time like this. Kennedy has the moral courage to stand up for what he knows is right. . . I've got a suitcase of votes, and I'm going to take them to Mr Kennedy and dump them in his lap.[6]

An extension of the sit-ins developed in the form of the 'Freedom Rides', which brought supporters from the north to join in the southern struggle. Multi-racial bus rides had been used before in civil rights campaigning,[7] but this time they met with bitter and violent resistance, and attracted widespread publicity. The Freedom Rides were organized by CORE, and Martin Luther King was elected Chairman of the Freedom Ride Co-ordinating Committee. In May 1961 six pairs of volunteers, black and white, left Washington DC aboard Greyhound and Trailways buses to travel through the Southern States.[8] Their main aim was to challenge the segregation of facilities at the waiting-rooms and lunch-counters of bus-terminals. In Alabama and Tennessee the Freedom Riders were savagely attacked by white mobs, including Ku Klux Klansmen, while local police did little to prevent the violence. Robert Kennedy, by this time the Attorney-General, sent nearly 700 US Marshals to provide the protection which the local authorities seemed reluctant to give. Martin King had protested bitterly at the failure of local law enforcement agencies to provide protection:

> The law may not be able to make a man love me, but it can keep him from lynching me.[9]

The Attorney-General requested a 'cooling-off period' from the Freedom Rides, Dr King rejected the request, but he did advise a 'temporary lull'. The Freedom Riders went ahead anyhow.

In November the Interstate Commerce Commission passed an order banning segregation in buses, trains, and supporting facilities, and Martin Luther King claimed this as 'the psychological turning point in our legal struggle'.[10]

In December of the same year Freedom Riders entered Albany, Georgia. Local blacks, led chiefly by the SNCC, responded to this with large-scale demonstrations of their own for the integration not only of bus and rail but also of other local facilities. Martin Luther King was asked to go and lend his influence to the struggle there – although a number of local blacks were unhappy at the invitation and the way in which, as they saw it, King's presence would bring too much media attention and make a national issue of what they saw as primarily a local one. During the campaign, many blacks were arrested and imprisoned, including Martin Luther King. Martin declared his intention of staying in prison for the cause. If convicted, he said, he would not pay his fine, and he warned his followers and friends that he expected to spend Christmas in prison. But on 18 December a compromise was agreed, and Martin Luther King left prison. Other demonstrators were released on bail, although the charges against them were not dropped. The compromise, which left local blacks and SNCC members most unhappy, involved the desegregation of terminal facilities whilst leaving buses, parks, libraries and cinemas segregated. Martin Luther King's part in this, as an outsider, was regarded by many as a disaster, and the *New York Herald Tribune* described it as 'one of the most stunning defeats of his career'.[11]

The campaign in Albany went on until August 1962, but had to be admitted a failure. In addition to the problems between local and national leadership which were undoubtedly a factor in the failure, it would seem that a tactical mistake had been made in attacking all the segregated facilities at once, instead of concentrating on just one or two. Albany underlined the importance for effective non-violent resistance of selecting the right means of protest aimed at the appropriate object and at the right time.

Other serious differences between black leaders came to the surface in the summer of 1962. Disagreements about how best to pursue the goal of a society free from racism had long existed between black American churchmen, and especially between the younger and the older church leaders. The views of the older leadership were exemplified by Joseph H. Jackson, the pastor of Olivet Baptist Church in Chicago, and since 1953 the President of the National Baptist Convention USA Inc. Joseph Jackson favoured a gradualist approach to the problems of blacks, and thought that the community's best chances lay in education and in helping individual blacks to obtain success in white society. He was conservative in theology, and his political views were dominated by a strong patriotism. He believed that what was good for America must in the long run be good for blacks. He was strongly opposed to the movements of non-violent resistance and civil disobedience as they developed (although he had been in favour of the Montgomery campaign). He argued that:

> the techniques of nonviolence and especially any form of civil disobedience breed lawlessness, violence, riots, bitterness, and the polarization of the races . . . Such methods, together with their inevitable consequences, threaten the efficacy of both the Christian gospel and genuine patriotism. His opposition to such techniques has been both adamant and consistent.[12]

Within the National Baptist Convention, however, were Martin Luther King and many of his supporters. The conflict between the King party and Joseph Jackson was out in the open from at least 1960. In September 1962 the young dissenters from conservative leadership and caution broke from the parent group to form the National Progressive Baptist Convention. Peter Paris, in his book *Black Leaders in Conflict*, writes about the causes of the split:

> Some hold tenaciously to the view that Jackson's tenure of office was the sole issue, while others believe that it was Jackson's moderation in committing the convention and himself to what was then called an active and militant stance regarding civil rights and how racism should be opposed. And there are some who reduce the whole issue to matters of petty jealousies,

personal egotism, and other personality traits of the two leaders.[13]

Certainly Joseph Jackson was highly critical of the sending of representatives from the Baptist Convention to join the protests in Albany:

> It is hypocrisy for a delegation to leave Chicago and go to Albany to fight segregation.[14]

The Albany campaign was a bad time for Martin Luther King. It did not achieve its objectives; it revealed rifts in the leadership of black civil rights leaders; and it brought into the open serious differences between black Christians as to how they should respond to the movements for racial justice.

1963 was to be a year of trial, but also a time of more positive progress. In March the SCLC began a campaign in Birmingham, Alabama, aimed at resisting the segregation of eating facilities in the town and protesting at the segregation maintained in shops and businesses. The campaign began with the familiar method of sit-ins, but two additional features developed. One was a deliberate SCLC policy to cripple businesses in Birmingham (particularly retail trade) during the Easter sales period by withholding black custom from stores which insisted on segregation. The second was the recruitment of 250 volunteers to train thousands of blacks in the techniques of non-violent resistance. The SCLC and Dr King were anxious to maintain a non-violent approach, but they recognized that this would be difficult in Birmingham. Indeed, Birmingham had been chosen for the campaign partly because it offered the possibility of direct confrontation with the most reactionary types of southern whites. The Commissioner of Public Safety in Birmingham was Eugene (Bull) Connor, an unimaginative man entirely opposed to Negro rights and unequivocal in his determination to use crude force to suppress the black movement. Martin Luther King and his supporters had realized that a vital factor in a successful civil rights campaign was the impression conveyed to the rest of America outside the Southern States through the media.[15] A campaign conducted in an area with an imaginative and reasonably liberal police chief was not likely to yield dramatic evidence of hard southern intransigence and white brutality which would move other Americans to indignant protest on behalf of ill-treated blacks. But the sight of Bull Connor and his police, knocking over non-violent demonstrators with powerful jets of water from the Fire Department's hoses, setting police dogs on to non-violent men and women, and beating and man-handling people who took the ill-treatment with quiet dignity was a powerful propaganda piece. Press and television reporters were present during the Birmingham campaign, and the television pictures especially were highly effective in arousing the consciences of Americans on behalf of the black demonstrators.[16] The success of the Birmingham campaign required two things, in addition to the basic injustice of the blacks' position: discipline among the demonstrators so that they would appear on television and in the press as reasonable, gentle people; and a crude and violent opponent who unwittingly would provide a caricature of the intransigence, unreasonableness, and violence of Southern whites in opposing the legitimate demands of their black fellow-citizens. President Kennedy was to say of Birmingham that the success of the civil rights movement owed as much to Bull Connor as it did to Abraham Lincoln.[17]

The Birmingham campaign was given the code letter C (for confrontation) by the SCLC. The aim was clear from the start. The resentment of local blacks at the failure of Birmingham to implement federal law on desegregation (Birmingham had closed the public parks rather than integrate them) was to be given expression; but Birmingham was also to be used as part of a national campaign.

At the beginning of the campaign Martin King employed his rhetorical talents to stir the black community.

> We shall march nonviolently. We shall force this nation, this city, this world, to face its own conscience. We will make the God of love in the white man triumphant over the Satan of segregation that is in him.[18]

Volunteers were asked to sign 'commitment cards' before engaging in demonstrations. The cards outlined ten 'commandments' for the non-violent demonstrators, including meditating daily on the teaching and life of Jesus; remembering that the movement sought justice and reconciliation rather than victory; refraining from 'the violence of fist, tongue, or heart'.[19]

On 12 April (Good Friday) Martin and his lieutenants deliberately engineered their own arrest. Martin was placed in solitary confinement. It was on 16 April that Martin wrote his famous and lengthy 'Letter from Birmingham Jail', a letter addressed to clergymen who had criticized his direct-action campaigns on the grounds that they would lead to violence and civil unrest. The letter is a moving testimonial to Martin's convictions about the rightness of non-violent direct action as the expression of Christian principles, and of his disappointment at the slowness of white Christians in the USA to appreciate the need to remove the injustices suffered by blacks:

My dear Fellow Clergymen,

While confined here in the Birmingham city jail, I came across your recent statement calling my present activities 'unwise and untimely.' . . . You deplore the demonstrations taking place in Birmingham. But your statement, I am sorry to say, fails to express a similar concern for the conditions that brought about the demonstrations. I am sure that none of you would want to rest content with the superficial kind of social analysis that deals merely with effects and does not grapple with underlying causes. It is unfortunate that demonstrations are taking place in Birmingham, but it is even more unfortunate that the city's white power structure left the Negro community with no alternative. . .

We have waited for more than 340 years for our constitutional and God-given rights. The nations of Asia and Africa are moving with jetlike speed toward gaining political independence, but we still creep at horse-and-buggy pace toward gaining a cup of coffee at a lunch counter. Perhaps it is easy for those who have never felt the stinging darts of segregation to say 'Wait' . . . when you see the vast majority of your twenty million Negro brothers smothering in an airtight cage of poverty in the midst of an affluent society . . . when you are humiliated day in and day out by nagging signs reading 'white' and 'coloured'; when your first name becomes 'nigger', your middle name becomes 'boy' (however old you are) and your last name becomes 'John', and your wife and mother are never given the respected title 'Mrs' . . . then you will understand why we find it difficult to wait. . .

I must make two honest confessions to you, my Christian and Jewish brothers. First, I must confess that over the past few years I have been gravely disappointed with the white moderate. I have almost reached the regrettable conclusion that the Negro's greatest stumbling block in his stride towards freedom is not the White Citizen's Counciler or the Ku Klux Klanner, but the white moderate, who is more devoted to 'order' than to justice; who prefers a negative peace which is the absence of tension to a positive peace which is the presence of justice; who constantly says, 'I agree with you in the goal you seek, but I cannot agree with your methods of direct action'; who pater-nalistically believes he can set the timetable for another man's freedom; who lives by a mythical concept of time and who constantly advises the Negro to wait for a 'more convenient season'. Shallow understanding from people of good will is more frustrating than absolute misunderstanding from people of ill will. . .

Let me take note of my other major disappointment. I have been so greatly disappointed with the white church and its leadership. Of course, there are some notable exceptions. . . But. . . I have been disappointed with the church. . . When I was suddenly catapulted into the leadership of the bus protest in Montgomery, Alabama, a few years ago, I felt we would be supported by the white church. I felt that the white ministers, priests, and rabbis of the South would be among our strongest allies. Instead, some have been outright opponents, refusing to understand the freedom movement and misrepresenting its leaders; all too many others have been more cautious than courageous and have remained silent. . .[20]

On 20 April, Martin Luther King was released from prison, and six days later was fined $50 and five days 'loss of liberty' (already served). But the marches continued. On 2 May, 950 children between the ages of six and sixteen were arrested, as 6000 people marched. The following day Bull Connor's patience gave way, and he ordered the police to use their dogs and their night-sticks on the demonstrators. Firemen were ordered to turn their hoses on them. The discipline of non-violence did not entirely hold. Some blacks began to retaliate, and young blacks who were not necessarily associated with the Christian *mores* of the majority began to hurl bricks and bottles at the police in response to the violence they suffered. But the majority of demonstrators re-mained non-violent in the face of great provocation. By 7 May more than 2000 had been arrested, and the city's resources were fully stretched to deal with them.

Finally, and after persuasion from the Attorney-General and the Federal authorities, the leaders of Birmingham came to an agreement with the demonstrators.[21] They agreed to release those who had been arrested during the course of the campaign (by the end the number had reached nearly 3000); to set up a bi-racial committee to prepare a timetable for desegregation in Birmingham; to increase the hiring of blacks on a non-discriminatory basis in the city's business and industry; and to desegregate lunch counters, rest rooms, fitting rooms, and drinking fountains.[22] The agreement met all the demands of the SCLC, and marked a notable victory for Martin Luther King. Not only had the campaign secured its aims in Birmingham; it had also had considerable impact upon the Federal Government. Lewis judged that as a result of the Birmingham campaign and its aftermath:

> The country was astir as never before since the Civil War over the dilemma of race. On June 11, John Kennedy, whose Administration belatedly rethought its priorities, spoke to the nation to advise that he was requesting Congress to enact immediately the most comprehensive civil rights bill to date. The President's speech was by far the most positive he had made on behalf of the American black.[23]

However, the solution to Birmingham's problems was not quite as simple as the agreement had suggested. Just a few hours after it was signed time-bombs exploded at the homes of black leaders (including the home of Martin's brother, A. D. King). The black community, especially the young and the poor, responded in riots which caused widespread destruction, and which were only brought to an end when the President despatched Federal troops to Birmingham. The President's decision to act more resolutely on racial matters presumably reflected concern at the violence in the South as well as the persuasiveness of the SCLC campaign. Nevertheless, Martin Luther King and his supporters had achieved much during a few months in Birmingham.

1963 was also the year of the march on Washington, which provided Martin King with the platform for one of his most famous speeches. The main aim of the march was to press Congress to pass a comprehensive civil rights law, but it also provided a clear example to the nation of the growing support for the civil rights movement. The march, which congregated on Washington on 28 August, was made up of an impressive cross-section of blacks and whites. In spite of the strictures on the white church contained in the Letter from Birmingham Jail – but also partly because of them – many white church leaders associated themselves with the civil rights movement in the summer of 1963. One such leader was Dr Eugene Carson Blake, later to become General Secretary of the World Council of Churches. Dr Blake told me how in 1963, when he was Stated Clerk of the Presbyterian Church in the USA, he was drawn almost accidentally into an association with the civil rights movement after Birmingham. The television coverage of the Birmingham campaign and the Letter from Birmingham Jail made him see the civil rights issue much more sharply and encouraged him to work for the involvement of the white churches in some aspects of the civil rights movement. He became Chairman of the Commission on Religion and Race of the National Council of Churches, and so was involved in the March on Washington.[24]

It is estimated that a quarter of a million people attended the march, and that more than 75,000 of them were white. Fourteen major religious, civic, and labour organizations participated in the march. Speeches were delivered by representatives of the participating groups, from Cardinal O'Boyle of the Washington Roman Catholic diocese to Walter Reuther of the Union of Automobile Workers, and including Eugene Carson Blake. Entertainers added their contribution, with ballads from Bob Dylan and songs from Joan Baez and Peter, Paul, and Mary.[25] But the climax came in a speech delivered from the Lincoln Memorial by Martin Luther King. The speech was punctuated, as his sermons and speeches so often were, by the enthusiastic comments and encouragement of the crowd, who responded to his great public utterances the way a black congregation was accustomed to respond to its preachers. Through the speech there ran the refrain, 'I have a dream'.

I have a dream that my four little children will one day live in a nation where they will not be judged by the color of their skin, but by the content of their character. I have a dream today![26]

The speech is full of colourful metaphors, supplemented by quotations from the Declaration of Independence, the prophet Isaiah, and concluding with the words of a Negro spiritual which four and a half years later were to be inscribed on his tombstone:

Free at last, Free at last. Thank God Almighty we're free at last.

Lewis describes it as 'rhetoric almost without content'. Certainly it was a speech which appealed to the emotions rather than the intellects of the crowd; yet this was after all, a southern Baptist preacher providing the inspiration for people in a hard struggle, at the end of a long day. The speech became and remained one of the famous and often quoted utterances of Martin Luther King. And the March on Washington was recognized as a symbol of the determination of a large part of the nation to see that civil rights should be clearly defined in legislation and upheld in everyday affairs throughout the nation. Hubert Humphrey, who was present, said:

> All this probably hasn't changed any votes on the civil rights bill, but it's a good thing for Washington and the nation and the world.[27]

Less than three months later any euphoria Martin may have felt after the March on Washington was dispelled by the assassination of President Kennedy; an ominous foreshadowing of his own death four and a half years later. But the assassination was to have an effect on the prospects for enacting civil rights legislation.

The emphasis of the civil rights movement in the period after Birmingham was on voter registration. One of the problems of blacks in the Southern States was that even although they were entitled to vote they were often not registered to do so. Officials in the South were often deliberately unco-operative, and made it as difficult as possible for blacks to register. In Alabama, Mississippi, and Louisiana local whites had effectively prevented blacks from registering to vote, using methods that included economic intimidation and the sacking of black employees.[28] But there were simpler ways of making it difficult for blacks to have their names entered on the voting registers. The Constitution required that an intending voter could be asked:

> to write an interpretation of any of the 285 sections of the document, write an essay 'on duties and obligations of a citizen under a republican form of government', and 'be of good moral character'. The decision on those three qualifications had been in the hands of the county voter registrar.[29]

Such requirements were applied with obvious partiality. For whites there was little or no difficulty in enrolling as a voter, regardless of their standard of literacy or their knowledge of the Constitution. For blacks, the situation was very different.

Selma, Dallas County, was at the heart of the black belt in Alabama. In the early 1960s its population of voting age consisted of 15,115 blacks and 14,400 whites. Yet of the 9877 people registered to vote in Selma, 9542 were white.[30] In order to register, an intending black voter was required:

> to fill in more than fifty blanks, write from dictation a part of the constitution, answer four questions about the governmental process, read four passages from the constitution and answer four questions on them. . .[31]

An enquiry of the US Commission on Civil Rights in Jackson, Mississippi, in 1965 showed that,

> many county registrars had discriminated against blacks through a number of devices such as: (*a*) more difficult constitutional sections to interpret; (*b*) insufficiencies in the completion of application forms; and (*c*) affording assistance to white applicants but not to blacks.[32]

As a consequence, in the period between May 1962 and August 1964, out of 1232 whites who applied for registration 945 were accepted, whereas out of 795 blacks who applied only 93 were accepted.

Selma appeared to be an obvious choice to begin a drive to register black voters. The Student Nonviolent Co-ordinating Committee had had workers in Selma to encourage registration since February 1963. But the campaign took on a new note of urgency and attracted national attention at the end of 1964 and during the first three months of 1965. In December 1964 Martin Luther King Jr went to Oslo to become the youngest ever recipient of the Nobel Peace Prize. The recognition afforded by that was a token of the increasing fame of Martin Luther King and the great respect in which he was held in many parts of America and around the world. It was also seen by Dr King as an acknowledgement of the justice of the cause of the American Negro in his struggle for civil rights. Soon after his return from Oslo Martin Luther King found himself in the very different environment of Selma, Alabama. The SCLC launched its own campaign to encourage voter registration, and on 1 January 1965 Martin King joined his fellow-workers there. Speaking at a meeting at Brown's Chapel Methodist Church in Selma on 2 January, he said:

> We are going to start a march on the ballot boxes by the thousands. We must be willing to go to jail by the thousands. We are not asking, we are demanding the ballot.[33]

The technique used in Selma was that of the mass march. Thousands of blacks would gather together, and then march to the courthouse, where they would ask to be registered.

The local sheriff, Jim Clark, vigorously opposed the demonstrations and the marchers. On 1 February Martin and 770 other marchers were arrested. Martin was released on February 5, but even so brief a period of imprisonment was sufficient to make a considerable impact on the world beyond Selma. The arrest of the Nobel Prizewinner made headlines across the world, and Martin

Luther King knew how to make use of that kind of publicity. From his prison he wrote:

> This is Selma, Alabama. There are more Negroes in jail with me than there are on the voting rolls.[34]

On Sunday, 7 March, a group of 525 people set out to march from Selma to Montgomery in order to dramatize their case and bring it directly to the attention of Governor George Wallace. The Governor, however, issued an order forbidding the march. At Edmund Pettus Bridge, on the outskirts of Selma, the marchers were met by state troopers who used night sticks and tear gas to beat back the peaceful procession. More than sixty people were treated for injuries back at the Parsonage of Brown's Chapel, and a further seventeen more seriously injured people were admitted to hospital.[35] The incident received widespread publicity, with newspapers giving the day the title of 'Bloody Sunday'. The publicity created widespread support for the Selma campaign. Liberal Americans were horrified by newspaper pictures and television reports of the violence perpetrated against peaceful demonstrators. Their indignation was strengthened by statements from the SCLC, whose vice-president Hosea Williams said:

> I fought in World War II and I once was captured by the German Army, and I want to tell you that the Germans never were as inhuman as the state troopers of Alabama.[36]

As a result of the publicity some 400 priests, ministers, and rabbis from all over the country congregated in Selma for a second march which Martin Luther King had called for 9 March.

The second march, swollen by out-of-state support, was much larger than the first. Several times the number of people who had participated in the first march set out two days later to make what they thought would be the fifty-four mile journey to Montgomery.[37] A request was made for Federal troops to protect the marchers, but the response of the Federal Government was to issue an injunction against the march. This posed a difficult problem for Martin Luther King. He had constantly appealed to Federal Government to support the rights of blacks when State Governments infringed those rights. Co-operation with Federal authority was an important part of his strategy. The Federal injunction, issued because it was felt that a cooling-down period was needed in Alabama, created a quandary. The second march had been planned; supporters from outside the state had been stirred up by the events of the first march, and had come to Selma determined to do something. Faced by this difficulty, Martin King appears to have settled for an awkward compromise which was to attract much criticism.

There seems to have been a pre-arranged plan that the marchers would go only as far as the Edmund Pettus Bridge, and that they would then turn and go back into Selma instead of proceeding on to the national highway and the road to Montgomery. But in a speech before the march set off Martin Luther King suggested that they were going all the way to Montgomery.

> We have the right to walk the highways, and we have the right to walk to Montgomery if our feet will get us there. I have no alternative but to lead a march from this spot to carry our grievances to the seat of Government. . . I would rather die on the highways of Alabama than make a butchery of my conscience.[38]

The three-thousand strong inter-racial group of marchers then set out through the streets of Selma. They crossed the bridge, and one mile beyond it were met by Alabama State Troopers blocking the highway. The order forbidding the march to continue was read; Martin asked for time for the marchers to pray, and this was granted. They all knelt in prayer, and as they rose the troopers were ordered to move back to the sides of the highway. The road to Montgomery was clear. At that moment Dr King instructed the marchers to turn back. Lewis points to the irony of the fact that as the demonstrators marched back to their starting point they were singing one of the favourite songs of the movement: 'Ain't Gonna Let Nobody Turn Me 'Round'.[39]

There seems to be little doubt that on this occasion Martin Luther King was confused in his strategy and misleading in statements he had about the capitulation to Federal authority. Lewis cites conflicting statements by King about the march, and suggests that he was influenced by his previous policy of appealing to Federal authority against disobeying a Federal injunction, and that he may also have been worried by rumours of Ku Klux Klan marksmen on the road to Montgomery.

> It would have been better if Martin had forthrightly confessed that he was unwilling to forfeit the cooperation of the federal establishment by defying a judicial injunction or that he gravely feared the savagery to the marchers by the police and the Klan.[40]

The weakness of this moment at Selma was picked upon by

Black Power critics of Martin Luther King. Eldridge Cleaver charged Martin with denying history 'a great moment, never to be recaptured'. And the incident strengthened the arguments of the Black Power enthusiasts, who felt that Martin's non-violence was not an effective answer to the entrenched power of whites. A few weeks earlier the Black Power leader, Malcolm X, had been assassinated in Harlem. The anonymous initial of Malcolm X reflected the view that since Negro slaves had had names given them by their white masters, the American Negro was without a true identity, and therefore had no name he could properly use. Malcolm X had been bitingly critical of Martin Luther King on many occasions. He asserted that whites were very happy to have non-violent black leaders like Martin King, and compared them with the 'house negroes' in the old days of slavery. The house negro, he said, would fight even harder than the master to save the house when it was burning down, whereas the 'field negro' would pray for the house to burn. So the non-violent civil rights leaders, he felt, were helping to preserve a system that would be better dealt with by destruction.

> . . . King is the best weapon that the white man . . . has ever gotten in this country, because he is setting up a situation where, when the white man wants to attack Negroes, they can't defend themselves, because King has put this foolish philosophy out – you're not supposed to fight or you're not supposed to defend yourself.[41]

Malcolm X did not share Martin King's confidence in the ability of America to secure full civil rights for blacks, nor did he accept the premise of the SCLC that the aim of civil rights agitation was to enable blacks to have a larger portion of the privileges of American society and to be part of the great American dream. For him, American society had to be dramatically changed before the black could expect justice and freedom within it.

> No, I'm not an American. I'm one of the 22 million black people who are the victims of Americanism. . . And I see America through the eyes of the victim. I don't see any American dream; I see an American nightmare.[42]

So Malcolm X saw a need for blacks to seize power; and his vigorous championing of this view helped create among blacks a more critical attitude to incidents in the campaigns of non-violent civil rights leaders that did not seem to yield results. The turn-around at the Edmund Pettus Bridge was one such incident.

However, the promised march to Montgomery did eventually take place. On 15 March, President Johnson announced that a Voting Rights Act would be introduced almost immediately. In the wake of this indication of Federal support, a vast crowd set out on 21 March on a triumphant walk from Selma to Montgomery. Some 8000 people spent several days on the journey, suitably refreshed along the way by meetings and speeches and songs. During part of the march Martin was away attending to affairs elsewhere, but he returned for the final day and led the great procession through the streets of the town from which he had set out on his own pilgrimage of civil rights campaigning nearly ten years earlier. In the grounds of the State Capitol he delivered one of his memorable speeches, encouraging the crowd with the promise that the civil rights campaign had become an irresistible movement that no power or opposition could now halt.

> I come to say to you this afternoon, however difficult the moment, however frustrating the hour, it will not be long, because truth pressed to earth will rise again. How long? Not long, because no lie can live for ever. How long? Not long, because you will reap what you sow. How long? Not long, because the arm of the moral universe is long, but it bends towards justice. How long? Not long. Because mine eyes have seen the glory of the coming of the Lord. . .[43]

The rhetoric was splendid, but not empty. The Selma campaign had achieved a great deal. It had led to an increase of blacks registered to vote. But it had also made an impact on the nation and on the progress of civil rights legislation in Washington. The Selma campaign appears to have attracted more support and sympathy in Congress than did the Birmingham campaign. Selma was more clearly non-violent, and focused sharper attention on the more limited issue of voting rights.[44] The passing of the Voting Rights Act of 1965 owed something to the events in Selma and the attention they had received. James Harvey's judgment was that

> Congress, while debating the voting rights bill, was greatly influenced by events in the South, especially those in Selma.[45]

The 1965 Act dealt with many of the problems that Negroes had been experiencing in the South. It suspended literacy tests for those registering to vote (President Johnson had observed that so far as Negroes were concerned 'even a college degree cannot be used to prove that he can read and write').[46] The Act gave the

Attorney General the power to appoint federal examiners to supervise voter registration in certain States, stipulated criminal penalties for interference with voter rights, and directed the Attorney General to institute proceedings against the use of State and local taxes as a qualification for voting. The Act was finally signed by President Johnson on 6 August 1965.[47]

It was now easier to establish the rights of Southern blacks to be on the voters' registers, but there was still a need to campaign for the implementation of those rights. Demonstrations continued into 1966 in the South to persuade blacks to register, and some of the marches were met with violence from whites who resented the inclusion of blacks on the voting registers regardless of what the law said. It was during the 1966 demonstrations that the phrase 'Black Power' first came to be used. In Grenada, Mississippi, Martin Luther King was joined by other black leaders in a march which led 1300 people to the courthouse to register. Stokely Carmichael, a militant black leader, encouraged the marchers to use the shout 'Black Power', and argued that civil rights marches should be made up of blacks only. 'We don't need any more white phonies and liberals invading our movement,' he said.[48] In singing the familiar civil rights song, 'We Shall Overcome', the marchers remained silent when they came to the line about 'Black and white together', and some even changed the main line of the lyric to 'We shall Overrun'. Some marchers took to wearing placards which bore the slogan, 'Move on Over or We'll Move on Over You'. Martin was disturbed by this evidence of the increasing appeal of black power. He was opposed to the philosophy of black power in seeking to establish a separation of black from white: he believed implicity in the need to establish a multi-racial community of blacks and whites reconciled to each other. And he was opposed to the idea of using violence in the civil rights struggle both on principle and because he regarded it as counter-productive. He was also worried by the use of 'Black Power' chants or slogans on marches in which he was involved, even when no violence was intended.

> I pleaded with the group to abandon the Black Power slogan. It was my contention that a leader has to be concerned about the problem of semantics. Each word, I said, has a denotative meaning . . . and a connotative meaning. . . Black Power carried the wrong connotations.[49]

Martin believed that to encourage blacks to think in terms of the possibility of violent revolt or retaliation was to damage severely their image in the eyes of white America (always important in the strategy of his campaigns of non-violent resistance), and to expose blacks to the possibility of violent retaliation which would far outweigh any gains that might be made. Violence he regarded as a misguided and impracticable tactic as well as something he believed to be wrong in principle.

In his book, *Chaos or Community?*, published in 1967, Martin Luther King wrote about his opposition to the black power movement.

> . . . besides opposing violence on principle, I could imagine nothing more impractical and disastrous than for any of us, through misguided judgment, to precipitate a violent confrontation in Mississippi. We had neither the resources nor the techniques to win . . . many Mississippi whites, from the government on down, would enjoy nothing more than for us to turn to violence in order to use this as an excuse to wipe out scores of negroes in and out of the march. . .[50]

He went on to say that few people suggested that negroes should not defend themselves when attacked, and he seemed to concur with the possibility of such self-defence. But, he wrote, the question was:

> whether it was tactically wise to use a gun while participating in an organized demonstration. If they lowered the banner of nonviolence, I said, Mississippi injustice would not be exposed and the moral issues would be obscured.

In 1966 Martin Luther King turned his attention for the first time to the northern cities and to economic questions. He was beginning to realize the wider implications of the things he believed in and campaigned for, and to recognize that the civil rights movement could not remain content with a narrow sphere of influence concerned with voters' rights and desegregation. To secure genuine justice for blacks it was necessary for them to have equality of opportunity in economic as well as political terms. Real reforms had been achieved, and much progress had been made, but the black still remained anchored firmly to the bottom of American society. To move up economically would involve challenges to the dominant white society which might be seen as even more demanding than desegregation. Martin observed:

> There are no expenses, and no taxes are required, for Negroes to share lunch counters, libraries, parks, hotels and other facilities with whites.[51]

But, he noted, better education and jobs for blacks, and the eradication of slums, would be expensive matters for American society to tackle. Dr King and the SCLC increasingly turned their attention to economic issues as they affected blacks throughout America. A new kind of campaign was launched, with the name Operation Breadbasket, aimed at securing jobs and better economic conditions for blacks. Negroes were asked to withdraw support from businesses that practised discrimination and to deal with firms that gave a fair share of jobs to blacks. Teams of clergy were organized to call on employers and obtain information about the numbers of negroes employed. They would then demand a fair share for negroes of all kinds of jobs, proportionate to the number of blacks in the community as a whole. Many employers co-operated willingly. When co-operation was refused, the clergy would call for an economic boycott of their businesses. The scheme produced impressive results. Dr King wrote of its application in his own home town:

> In Atlanta, Georgia, for instance, the Negroes' earning power has been increased by more than $20 million annually over the past three years through a carefully disciplined program of selective buying and negotiation by the Negro ministers.[52]

The new interest in economic issues concentrated attention especially upon the northern cities. These had had no part in the campaigns over desegregation and voting rights, yet many blacks in the North lived in situations of great poverty and deprivation. It was clear that there was still a great distance to be travelled before real justice could be achieved for the American Negro.

The other great issue that commanded Martin Luther King's attention from 1966 onwards was the Vietnam War. There are two reasons why in retrospect it seems entirely logical for him to have extended his concern for justice and peace to the situation in Vietnam. One was that his espousal of non-violence, even although he was not a thoroughgoing pacifist, made him uneasy about the use of vast resources of American power against the Vietnamese, especially when American bombers were attacking civilian targets. Secondly, issues of colour prejudice and white superiority were never far below the surface in discussion of the Vietnamese War. A far higher proportion of black troops than white were enlisted to fight in Vietnam. Blacks were less likely to be excluded from the draft because fewer of them were in college or in reserve occupations. But the black leadership generally in the United States was not anxious to support Martin on this issue.

The SCLC board voted that when Martin commented on the war he should not be regarded as speaking for the SCLC but as a private citizen.[53] The SCLC then, as now, saw the objectives of civil rights in terms of blacks joining the great American society. With such an aim it was one thing to criticize white Americans for preventing blacks exercising their privileges in society; quite another to suggest that blacks did not want to defend what the majority still saw as 'American interests' in SE Asia. In August 1980 I interviewed an official of the SCLC in Atlanta, and found a similar ambivalence.[54] I was told that the SCLC was in favour not only of non-violence but also of pacifism, since this was regarded as consistent with the teaching of Jesus. I then asked if that meant that the SCLC was opposed to the American arms programme and the re-introduction of the draft. Not at all, I was told. We blacks have a responsibility to share in the defence of our national sovereignty.

Martin's criticism of government policy towards Vietnam led to a deterioration of his relationship with President Johnson, who had done much to secure the passing of domestic legislation on civil rights. This was one of the consequences feared by moderate civil rights leaders. But it seemed to Martin a matter of conscience that he should speak out against the barbarities of the Vietnam War. He complained that America applauded non-violence when practised by blacks in America, but also applauded the sending of blacks to be violent in Vietnam.[55]

One of Martin Luther King's striking speeches on the Vietnam war was delivered at Riverside Church, New York, still a notable centre of resistance to the arms race and the draft.[56] He pointed to the consistency of his position in the civil rights struggle and his attitude to the war:

It would be very inconsistent of me to teach and preach non-violence in this situation and then applaud violence when thousands and thousands of people, both adults and children, are being maimed and mutilated and many killed in this war.[57]

He called for a negotiated end to the war, and suggested a five-point programme for achieving peace: an end to all bombing, north and south; the declaration of a unilateral cease-fire to prepare a climate for negotiation; a curtailment of military build-ups throughout South East Asia; realistic acceptance of the National Liberation Front; and establishment of a definite date by which all foreign troops would be withdrawn from Vietnam.[58] Even his critical biographer admitted that Martin's statements on Vietnam revealed 'a political maturity and courage possessed by no other national civil rights leader and . . . unexpressed by the great majority of national political leaders'.[59]

The stand against the Vietnam War impressed young blacks in the United States, including many who had serious reservations about the efficacy of Martin Luther King's earlier campaigns of non-violent resistance. In speaking out on national issues Dr King alienated some of his long-time supporters and jeopardized his relationship with the Government. But at the same time he evoked the support and approval of young idealists who were grateful to see a leader of his reputation standing up for what they so clearly saw to be right. The feeling has persisted. At Princeton in the summer of 1980 I spoke to young black graduate students who had great admiration for Martin Luther King. For them, although they had been children when Dr King died, he above all black leaders epitomized the struggle for justice which they saw as still continuing and still urgent. They had reservations about his non-violence, for they were not sure that his methods could be effective now (although like many black Americans, they did not appreciate the distinctions between Gandhian non-violence and Christian pacifism). But they were impressed above all by the way in which Dr King in his last years had addressed himself clearly to the economic problems of blacks and to Vietnam. For the articulate and intelligent blacks who had grown up accepting as natural the benefits won in the struggles of the 1950s and 1960s, the identification as early as 1966 of what they now see as urgent problems for their people was evidence of Martin Luther King's greatness.

However, a concern with national issues did not prevent Martin King from continuing to be involved in the day-to-day problems of blacks in the Southern States. In February 1968 there was a strike by black sanitation workers in Memphis on an issue related to differences in the treatment of black and white sanitation workers. An all-out stoppage was called for on 28 March, and Martin agreed to lead a march on that day. On the fringes of the march violence erupted among black youths, who broke shop windows and struggled with the police. The violence was another illustration of the tensions within the civil rights movement between those who accepted the non-violent techniques of Dr King and those who had grown impatient with the peaceful approach. Dr King was upset by the violence, and determined to prove that such a march could be held in Memphis without violence. He suggested a second march on 8 April, and seems to have accepted that he and his close aides would have a far greater say in the arrangements for that day. A meeting to plan the march was arranged in Memphis for 4 April. The evening before a meeting was held at the Mason Temple and Martin Luther King delivered the major speech. In retrospect, the speech appears to reveal an uncanny awareness of what was to come. He spoke of threats that had been made against his life. Threats and violent action against him were no new thing. And yet that night Martin King spoke of them with an almost morbid preoccupation.

> Like anybody, I would like to live a long life. Longevity has its place. But I'm not concerned about that now. I just want to do God's will. And He's allowed me to go up to the mountain. And I've looked over, and I've seen the promised land.[60]

Less than twenty-four hours later, Martin Luther King was preparing to go out for a meal with a friend. He stepped out for a moment on to the balcony of the Lorraine Motel, where he had been staying. From a room of a small hotel at the back of the Lorraine, a shot rang out. Martin Luther King Jr had been assassinated. The assassin was James Earl Ray, a small-time criminal whose only motive appears to have been a desire to achieve fame as a criminal celebrity.[61] He was arrested two months later, on 8 June, at London Airport, and after trial committed to the maximum security area of Tennessee State Prison.

To his friends, to people across the nation, and to admirers around the world, the death of Martin Luther King at the age of thirty-nine was a great shock and a profound loss. Yet as with Mahatma Gandhi and many other martyrs to a cause, the death of Martin King was a testimony to his commitment to the causes in which he was willing to sacrifice his life. It was tragic and yet somehow also fitting.

In a tribute delivered at the funeral at Ebenezer Baptist Church, Atlanta, on 9 April, Martin King's former teacher, Dr Harold DeWolf, said:

> Amid the tempestuous seas and treacherous storms of injustice, hate and violence which threatened the very life of mankind, his faith was a solid, immovable rock. He received hundreds of threats upon his life, yet for thirteen years he walked among them unafraid. His single commitment was to do God's will for him; his trust was in God alone.
>
> On that rock of faith God raised in him a lighthouse of hope. No white backlash nor black backlash could cause him to despair. He dreamed a dream of world brotherhood, and unlike

most of us he gave himself absolutely to work for the fulfilment of this inspired hope. He loved all men. Even the hate-filled foe of all he represented he tried sympathetically to understand.

He sought to relieve the slavery of the oppressors as well as that of the oppressed. . .[62]

There was a negative response to Martin King's death as riots broke out across the nation among blacks enraged by his assassination. There was also a positive response, in the acceleration of another piece of civil rights legislation. The Civil Rights Act of 1968 was passed on 10 April and signed on 11 April, just one week after the death of Martin Luther King Jr.

Martin Luther King's Understanding of Gandhian Non-Violence

The name of Martin Luther King has become indissolubly linked with the precepts and practices of a peaceful approach to situations of conflict. The Nobel Prize for Peace recognized the way in which Dr King had become a symbol of peace and reconciliation. His speeches, his books, and above all his actions, constantly emphasized the value he attributed to non-violence, and he provided a striking contrast with the more violent attitudes of other well-known black leaders in the civil rights movement.

Many people now seem to regard Martin King as an outstanding example of a Christian pacifist who demonstrated the effectiveness of pacifism. In July and August 1980 I talked to many people who had known Martin Luther King and to others who would regard themselves as his followers in the American civil rights movement today. I was struck by the facile way in which many of them regarded Dr King as a pacifist, and pacifism as the only appropriate Christian attitude to conflict. I have already mentioned the view expressed by an official of the SCLC, who told me that his organization was in favour of pacifism and also in favour of supporting the American defence programme.[1] Martin Luther King Sr described his son as a pacifist, although in common with others he did not appear to appreciate the subtleties of the Gandhian approach or the difference between Gandhian non-violence and pacifism.[2] What, then, was the view of Martin Luther King Jr on pacifism? One person who did suggest that Martin King was not a thoroughgoing pacifist was his one-time teacher, Dr Harold DeWolf.[3] And Dr King's writings suggest an attitude less thoroughgoing than the word pacifism demands.

However, it is evident that pacifism has been used somewhat loosely in the civil rights movement in the USA, and so it seems necessary to clear the ground by referring to definitions. Gandhi refused to use pacifism as a description of his approach to conflict because he was aware of the negative connotations of the word. He wished to emphasize the positive aspect of a resistance to evil which was active even though it was non-violent. And so the term *satyagraha* was coined in order to convey the impression of a determined struggle for truth and justice. Surely he was right in his perception of the largely negative impression which the word pacifism conveys. Historically, pacifism has been used to describe a variety of attitudes from a complete refusal to use physical force against an opponent or to engage in any kind of warfare, to a concern to establish peace whilst not ruling out the possibility of using the restraining power of physical force. So expressions such as 'complete pacifism' or 'thoroughgoing pacifism' come to be used to express the more extreme view. Recent discussion, however, has come to distinguish between two words describing two significantly different attitudes.

For example, Martin Ceadel defines pacifism as the view that war is always wrong, and should never be resorted to, whatever the consequences of refraining from fighting.[4] He points out that the slightly different word pacificism has been used by A. J. P. Taylor and others to describe a less extreme view, that war, although sometimes necessary, is always an irrational and inhumane way of solving disputes, and its prevention should always be an over-riding political priority. Pacificism, then, makes the pursuit of peace the dominant concern, but does not rule out the possibility of the use of force in some circumstances. In Ceadel's words, pacificism 'sees the prevention of war as its main duty and accepts that however upsetting to the purists' conscience, the controlled use of force may be necessary to achieve this'.[5] So in Weber's terms pacifism is seen as an 'ethic of ultimate ends' and pacificism as an 'ethic of responsibility'. This has the advantage of retaining for pacifism the meaning it appears to have in popular usage, that to engage in war is always wrong. Such a definition is supported by another recent and fascinating study, *The Ethics of War*, by Barrie Paskins and Michael Dockrill. Their definition runs:

> A person is a pacifist if they have beliefs such that, if they acted in the way those beliefs require, they would refuse all participation in war.[6]

This definition of pacifism I accept and use; the definition of pacificism given by Ceadel also seems to me to be useful, and will be referred to in what follows.

In the light of these definitions I would argue that on the evidence available to us Martin Luther King Jr cannot be regarded as a pacifist. He had a deep and genuine commitment to non-violence, on the Gandhian pattern, and was opposed to the use of violence in any circumstances in the American civil rights movement. He also considered the use of violence in the civil rights struggle to be tactically unwise. It was only towards the end of his life that he began to apply his thinking on non-violence to a wider context, and in that wider context his thought was still in the process of being formed. It would be idle to speculate about the views Martin Luther King might have developed had he lived beyond his thirty-nine years (he died at the age Gandhi was at when, in 1908, he was still far from the end of his South African campaign). Whether or not Martin King would have come eventually to a pacifist position we do not know. Pacificism is a word that might more justly be applied to his views so far as they had developed by 1968. But above all, Martin King was a Christian who accepted the validity of the Gandhian techniques of non-violent resistance, and who wedded *satyagraha* to the Christian concept of *agape*.

It was at Crozer Theological Seminary that Martin Luther King began what he described as a 'serious intellectual quest for a method to eliminate social evil'.[7] His starting point, of course, was the teaching of Jesus and the interpretation of that in Christian tradition, but his initial conclusion was that the ethics suggested by Jesus could only be effective in individual relationships. Then he heard Dr Mordecai Johnson lecture on Gandhi, and was so moved by what he heard that he went out and bought half-a-dozen books on Gandhi's life and work. Through the eyes of a Hindu he saw certain aspects of the Christian faith in a new way. What he read led him to a reassessment of his interpretation of the ethic of Jesus, and he concluded that he had been quite wrong to have regarded the teaching of Jesus as applicable only to individual relationships.[8] What Gandhi had done for his understanding of Jesus he believed could be done for others, for he regarded Gandhi as the first person in history to have 'lifted the love ethic of Jesus above the individual level'.

After reading Gandhi, Martin King turned to the Christian theologian, Reinhold Niebuhr. Niebuhr had at one time been a pacifist and in the early 1930s was a member of the Fellowship of

Reconciliation, a Christian pacifist organization. He was acquainted with the Gandhian methods used in India, and as early as 1932 Niebuhr had suggested that Gandhi's techniques were particularly appropriate to the struggle for racial equality in America.[9] But Niebuhr had turned away from pacifism. In order to create a more Christian society, Niebuhr said, it is necessary to change social structures; moral ideals alone will not do. So far as peace and war are concerned, he came to regard pacifism as unrealistic precisely because he saw it as an abrogation of responsibility and a withdrawal from the arena of hard political debate and action.[10] His views were influential, and discouraged many from following the path of Christian pacifism. Martin King acknowledged the help he gained from his reading of Niebuhr, who enabled him to appreciate the complexities of man's social involvement and the importance of power structures and collective action in securing or impeding the implementation of moral ideals.[11] It was Niebuhr's influence that led Martin to the conclusion that many pacifists had 'an unwarranted optimism concerning man'.[12] This in turn prevented Martin King from joining a pacifist organization, a significant indication of his hesitancy about absolute pacifism. William R. Miller concluded that after his reading of Niebuhr,

> Martin remained a theological liberal, but he felt that he emerged from his study of Niebuhr with a more realistic kind of pacifism, free from the perfectionist optimism that had troubled him in Rauschenbusch and others.[13]

Martin Luther King's reading of Niebuhr was critical, however, and he thought he detected inadequacies in Niebuhr's position. It seemed to King that Niebuhr interpreted pacifism as passive non-resistance to evil, and lacked a true appreciation of the potential of non-violent methods for resisting injustice and oppression. Nevertheless, the important point to note here is that the influences of both Gandhi and Niebuhr worked upon Martin while he was at Crozer, encouraging him to glimpse some of the possibilities of non-violent methods for securing social change; enabling him to see that simplistic solutions are not likely to be adequate in matters relating to complex social structures; and dissuading him from making a personal commitment to a pacifist organization in spite of his assessment of the importance of non-violence.

Martin Luther King had thought about the theory of non-violent action. Soon after his arrival in his first pastorate in Montgomery, his theorizing was put to the test in the events surrounding the bus-boycott. In the book that gave his view of the Montgomery campaign, Dr King admitted his debt to Thoreau's ideas of civil disobedience. He had read Thoreau's 'Essay on Civil Disobedience' whilst a student at Morehouse many years before.[14] When he was propelled into leadership of the bus-boycott Martin King was struck by the aptness of Thoreau's ideas for the situation in Montgomery. Thoreau, whose thought had also influenced Mahatma Gandhi, had been imprisoned in 1846 for refusing to pay a poll tax. He refused payment because he was unwilling to offer any support to a state that sanctioned slavery. The idea that a citizen had a duty to disobey unjust laws had an obvious application to the civil rights movement, and was especially appealing where, as in the southern states, local laws relating to segregation were at odds with Federal law. Martin Luther King described his reading of the 'Essay on Civil Disobedience' at Moorhouse as his 'first intellectual contact with the theory of nonviolent resistance',[15] and Thoreau was an important influence in his developing ideas of how civil disobedience could be used to help the struggle of the Negro.

The other seminal idea in Martin King's mind at the beginning of the Montgomery boycott was the Christian concept of *agape*. In many of his sermons and several of his books King refers to the different words the Greek New Testament has for 'love':[16] *eros*, for sexual love; *philia*, for brotherly affection; and *agape*, a word developed in New Testament usage to describe a particular concept of a sacrificial, sympathetic, caring love for all people. *Agape* is well described in Paul's First Letter to the Corinthians:

> Love is patient; love is kind and envies no one. Love is never boastful, nor conceited, nor rude; never selfish, not quick to take offence. Love keeps no score of wrongs; does not gloat over other men's sins, but delights in the truth.[17]

This Christian ideal of love was very important to Martin Luther King. It was for him the clearest and most compelling expression of a love which moved him to stand up for justice on behalf of the segregated and humiliated Negro of the South, and at the same time discouraged him from hating the white man who was his adversary in the battle. As a Christian minister Martin Luther King believed that *agape* was not only defined in the New Testament but also exemplified in the life of Jesus, and in his forgiveness of those who persecuted him.

The way in which the New Testament concept of *agape* and Thoreau's ideas on civil disobedience worked together in Martin

King's mind is seen in his anticipation of his speech at the beginning of the Montgomery bus-boycott on 5 December 1955. In a hasty review of what he might say, he thought:

> I would seek to arouse the group to action by insisting that their self-respect was at stake and that if they accepted such injustices without protesting, they would betray their own sense of dignity and the eternal edicts of God Himself. But I would balance this with a strong affirmation of the Christian doctrine of love.[18]

In the speech itself he said:

> . . . we come here tonight to be saved from that patience that makes us patient with anything less than freedom and justice.[19]

But the call for a revolt in the name of justice was carefully tempered by an insistence on the overriding importance of the ideal of Christian love:

> Love must be our regulating ideal. Once again we must hear the words of Jesus echoing across the centuries: 'Love your enemies, bless them that curse you, and pray for them that despitefully use you.'[20]

And reflecting later upon the ideals that inspired the boycott, he wrote:

> It was the Sermon on the Mount, rather than a doctrine of passive resistance, that initially inspired the Negroes of Montgomery to dignified social action.[21]

But as the boycott went on, he became increasingly aware of the appropriateness of Gandhi's methods:

> As the days unfolded, however, the inspiration of Mahatma Gandhi began to exert its influence. I had come to see early that the Christian doctrine of love operating through the Gandhian method of nonviolence was one of the most potent weapons available to the Negro in his struggle for freedom. . . Christ furnished the spirit and motivation, while Gandhi furnished the method.[22]

Gandhi's methods were studied and applied in regular training sessions during the Montgomery campaign, but the spirit as well as the techniques of Gandhian non-violent resistance were echoed in Montgomery as the black community were told:

> Our aim must never be to defeat or humiliate the white man, but to win his friendship and understanding.[23]

Martin King adopted some phrases from Gandhi without necessarily accepting the ideas that lay behind them. For example, during the Montgomery campaign he urged his followers to counter physical force with 'soul force'. In Gandhi's thought soul force was an essential ingredient of non-violence, but was related essentially to the idea that spiritual power and moral influence must eventually triumph over physical power. Gandhi's perception of body-force as inferior to soul-force was strongly coloured by his Hindu background, and was bound up with his ascetic life-style. We have seen how, for Gandhi, the struggle to establish the superiority of soul-force led to the rejection of the enjoyment of many of the normal physical pleasures of life, such as sex, good food, and elegant dress.[24] Martin King was entirely different from Gandhi in this respect, and he showed no signs of wishing to embrace what Gandhi himself meant by soul-force. As one American interpreter wrote of Martin Luther King:

> He felt no need to give up smart attire, good food or sex in order to be effectively non-violent.[25]

M. M. Thomas argued that Martin Luther King is also to be distinguished from Gandhi in his approach to power. Gandhi regarded political, social, or economic power as always inherently corrupting, and moral power, the power of ideas and ideals, as the only pure form of power. King, on the other hand, recognized a legitimate place for the exercise of power and wished to achieve and use power.

> Martin Luther King sees the non-violent movement as a movement of power-politics for the democratisation of power. It is power-politics itself, but one in which power and morality go together.[26]

Martin King's concept of soul force, then, was not Gandhian, but simply a way of expressing the need for unarmed people to stand up to the abusive power of a hostile police and civil authority with courage and determination. But King was always quite clear about the desirability of blacks in America winning and exercising power. His reading of Niebuhr had left him in no doubt about the need to change social structures in order to give clearer expression to Christian social values in society. The Christian, he believed, had to learn to combine love with the effective exercise of power.

> Power without love is reckless and abusive, and love without power is sentimental and anaemic.[27]

In spite of this difference between King and Gandhi (a difference of which Martin King was probably quite unaware), the experience of the Montgomery campaign led to a remarkably close approximation between Martin King and Mahatma Gandhi. In *Stride Toward Freedom*, Martin Luther King outlines the understanding of non-violence which was accepted in Montgomery.

First, he wrote, 'it must be emphasized that nonviolent resistance is not a method of cowards; it does resist. If one uses this method because he is afraid or merely because he lacks the instruments of violence, he is not truly nonviolent.'[28] He had learned from Gandhi's writings the difference between a 'passive resistance' which amounted to doing nothing, and an active resistance to evil which required all the more courage for being non-violent.

Secondly, he thought of non-violence as an approach which 'does not seek to defeat or humiliate the opponent, but to win his friendship and understanding'.[29] At the end of a non-violent campaign, he believed, there should be greater understanding, respect, and even love between those who had opposed each other, whereas in a violent campaign one could expect victory to be accompanied by bitterness and resentment.

Thirdly, and still closely in line with Mahatma Gandhi, he emphasized that the non-violent campaign directed its attack against the 'forces of evil rather than against persons who happen to be doing the evil. . . We are out to defeat injustice and not white persons who may be unjust.'[30]

A fourth characteristic was seen to be the willingness to accept suffering, if need be. For Gandhi the *Bhagavad Gita*'s teaching on *nishkama karma* served to encourage the notion that one should accept suffering in the causes of truth and *dharma*. For Martin King, it was the New Testament idea that suffering can be redemptive that justified the willing acceptance of imprisonment or violence on the part of the non-violent resister.

To these four foundations for non-violent resistance Martin Luther King added the principle of love, or *agape*, and the conviction that 'the universe is on the side of justice'. Both were much more closely related to Martin King's Christian background than to Gandhianism, and the last point was supported for Martin by his belief in a personal God. The non-violent resister 'knows that in his struggle for justice he has cosmic companionship'.[31]

Martin Luther King emerged from the Montgomery experience with a deep and genuine commitment to non-violence on the Gandhian pattern, and a conviction that it would be wrong to use violence in any circumstances that might arise in the civil rights movement in the United States. He had not had the opportunity to consider the wider implications of his philosophy of non-violence.

During the 1960s, however, Martin Luther King showed increasing interest in the relevance of Gandhian style non-violence to broader issues of peace and war. Two events outside the civil rights movement appear to have contributed to this. One was his journey to Oslo in December 1964 to receive the Nobel Peace Prize, and his awareness that by that award he had been recognized as an international spokesman for peace. The other was the beginning of the Vietnam War, and the special challenge that war presented to a leader of black Americans. Vietnam provided a particularly cruel example of the disparities between the treatment of blacks and whites in American society. Because blacks predominated in the less affluent and less well-educated segments of society, they were less likely to obtain exemption from the draft. A far higher proportion of blacks than whites served in Vietnam.[32]

Martin Luther King was one of the first well-known Christian leaders in the USA publicly to oppose the war in Vietnam. His opposition was deliberate and carefully thought out, and pursued in spite of his recognition of the risks such a public stand created for his work in the civil rights movement. When he was considering what he should say on Vietnam, Martin telephoned Dr Harold DeWolf and the two met over dinner to discuss the issue.[33] Martin acknowledged the danger of losing public support and respect in the United States by taking a stand on so controversial an issue, but in such a matter he would rather have been right than have won some lesser battle in the civil rights movement.

But even before Oslo and the Nobel Prize, Martin Luther King's thoughts had been moving towards the application of his philosophy of non-violence to wider issues. His book, *Why We Can't Wait*, published in 1964, contained an account of his reflections on the Birmingham campaign, and ended with the sentence:

> Nonviolence, the answer to the Negroes' need, may become the answer to the most desperate need of all humanity.[34]

The theme is also found in *Strength to Love*, a collection of sermons published in September 1963. At the end of that book is a chapter, 'Pilgrimage to Nonviolence', which had not been a sermon but was included at the request of his publishers because it provided an up-to-date account of his ideas on non-violence. After writing about some of the background to the development of his ideas on non-violent resistance and its use in the USA, he wrote:

> More recently I have come to see the need for the method of nonviolence in international relations. Although I was not yet convinced of its efficacy in conflicts between nations, I felt that while war could never be a positive good, it could serve as a negative good by preventing the spread and growth of an evil force. War, horrible as it is, might be preferable to surrender to a totalitarian system. But I now believe that the potential destructiveness of modern weapons totally rules out the possibility of war ever again achieving a negative good. If we assume that mankind has a right to survive, then we must find an alternative to war and destruction. In our day of space vehicles and guided ballistic missiles, the choice is either nonviolence or non-existence.[35]

His own position with regard to pacifism is expressed in that chapter:

> I am no doctrinaire pacifist, but I have tried to embrace a realistic pacifism which finds the pacifist position as the lesser evil in the circumstances. I do not claim to be free from the moral dilemmas that the Christian nonpacifist confronts, but I am convinced that the church cannot be silent while mankind faces the threat of nuclear annihilation. If the church is true to her mission, she must call for an end to the arms race.[36]

How, then, are we to understand the distinction between a 'doctrinaire pacifist' and 'realistic pacifism'? To do so we need to go back to the definitions of pacifism and pacificism. The position expressed by Martin Luther King is not that any kind of war is always wrong and should never be resorted to whatever the circumstances, but that the pursuit of war in particular ways – that is, by the use of weapons of mass destruction – is wrong. To make a distinction between these two positions may appear to be mere prevarication. But I shall argue in the next chapter that there are important consequences of a choice between an absolute pacifism which refuses the use of physical force against an opponent in any circumstances, and a pacificism which seeks to find effective alternatives to modern war.

So far as his thought had progressed, the indication appears to be that Martin King did not rule out the controlled use of force in some circumstances in order to create or maintain peace. He regarded the use of violence in the civil rights movement as wrong, partly because he believed that violence in such a struggle would foster hatred and bitterness which would long outlast any solution and could not contribute to the ultimate creation of a harmonious inter-racial community; and he opposed violence in that movement partly because he thought it tactically unwise.[37] He opposed American intervention in Vietnam because, as many other liberal Americans later acknowledged, it was extremely difficult to regard Vietnam as a 'just' war, and because he saw Vietnam demanding unfair sacrifices of American Negroes and encouraging blacks to be violent and destructive in an Asian country ostensibly in order to defend liberties for others which segregation denied the black American in his own country. By the time of his death he was also coming to an appreciation of the dilemmas posed to the Christian conscience by nuclear war. How his thought might have progressed after 1968 we cannot know.

The emphasis of Martin Luther King on non-violence was very similar to that of Gandhi. Non-violent resistance was seen to be an active and courageous opposition to injustice which was determined not to sit quietly and allow tyranny to go unchallenged, but which fought for the good of ally and enemy alike. For both of them, non-violent resistance was a positive concept, and offered a method of pursuing revolution by peaceful means. M. M. Thomas has written of Gandhi:

> Lenin and Gandhiji have been the most creative strategists of social revolution in the modern world – one advocating a strategy of violence and the other of non-violence. The future of a strategy which achieves the human ends of the revolution may well lie with Gandhism restated for our age on the basis of a doctrine of the spiritual significance of the body for man's existence and salvation, and of power in human relations, which is sounder than what lies behind Gandhism as we understand it from the writings of Gandhi and his followers.[38]

A combination of the insights and methods of Gandhi and King puts us well on the road to achieving such a strategy.

One final matter of comparison demands comment. There are some marked similarities between the experiences of Mahatma Gandhi and Martin Luther King which are important for a balanced assessment of their techniques of non-violent resistance.

Both came to adopt methods of non-violent resistance in attempts to counter racial prejudice. For Gandhi, it was the discrimination suffered by Indians in South Africa that led him to his formulation of *satyagraha*; for King, the disabilities imposed upon blacks in the Southern States of the USA encouraged his adaptation of Gandhian methods there.

Both of them were aware of working within a legal framework which seemed to promise eventual justice, and which provided an authority to which they could appeal against local abuses. During the South African struggle, Gandhi attached considerable importance to the overriding authority of the British Empire. In opposing policies of the Governments of Natal and the Transvaal he was always conscious of the possibility of appeal to Government in London. As we have seen, his support for Britain and the cause of the Empire in the Boer War and the First World War were coloured by this factor. In India Gandhi operated within a very different situation, but was still able on occasion to take advantage of the different pressures which were exerted on the Government of India in Delhi and Simla and those affecting parliament in London. And independence, when it came, clearly owed much to the election of a Labour Government in 1945. Martin Luther King was always very conscious of the conflict between local and state laws on segregation on the one hand and federal laws on the other. The relationship forged between the Kings and the Kennedys was an important part of this. Some of the major successes of the civil rights movement were the result of the Federal Government imposing its will upon recalcitrant local authorities.

Another element related to this, and important to both Gandhi and King, was the use both men made of mass communication and appeals to a wide public audience. For Gandhi his own newspapers, *Young India* and *Harijan*, were important methods of disseminating his opinions among his followers and of training them in the arts of *satyagraha*. The *Collected Works* of Mahatma Gandhi run to sixty-seven volumes and testify to the enormous amount of writing he completed. Most of this is in the forms of correspondence and weekly articles in his own papers. In addition to this, Mahatma Gandhi deliberately adopted a style of dress and a simplicity of life which symbolized his political message in a very effective way and appealed to a wide audience throughout India. Martin Luther King was acutely aware of the importance of the media in his campaigns in America. In order to exert pressure on hard-line Southern whites it was necessary to enlist the sympathy of whites of more liberal persuasion in other parts of the United States. Television coverage and press photographs which showed non-violent black demonstrators being abused, beaten, and degraded by Southern whites was one of the most effective ways of achieving this.

Mahatma Gandhi and Martin Luther King also had in common their use of religious symbols and sentiments to enlist support for their political campaigns. Both men were sincere in their own religious convictions, and there was nothing hypocritical in their use of religion. Nevertheless, religion played an essential part in their achievements. Mahatma Gandhi became an all-India leader in a way that no other Congress member could through his extraordinary ability to speak simply yet evocatively to the religious sensibilities of Hindu India. *Satyagraha* was based firmly on religious belief and principles. Gandhi made constant references to the *Bhagavad Gita* and to Hindu concepts of *karma* and *dharma*. He exemplified in his life-style the fastidious concern for vegetarianism, celibacy, and fasting which has important religious connotations in neo-Hinduism. Indeed, the very success of his appeal to religious sentiment led in the end to Gandhi's greatest failure by persuading many Muslims that the Ram Raj of Gandhi's dream would be an impossible condition for Muslims in an independent India.

Martin Luther King also spoke in a religious context and appealed to religious sentiment in a way that would be impossible in Western Europe. The language of his speeches and more especially the manner of his delivery closely reflected his background as a Southern Baptist preacher. The movement that he led was clearly a religious movement, and whether he spoke in a church or a public hall he could expect his speeches to be punctuated by the 'Amens' and the echoing shouts that are a feature of the black churches of the Southern states. So his speeches were laced with biblical phrases. In some of his great speeches there are repetitions of phrases which at first have some content – 'I have a dream that one day . . . sons of former slaves and sons of former slave owners will be able to sit down together at the table of brotherhood' – and then slide into biblical or other religious language which in the context of the speech often has no precise meaning – 'I have a dream that one day "every valley shall be exalted and every hill and mountain shall be made low".' The cadences were magnificent in their effect, but would have sounded slightly ridiculous in a non-religious environment. For Martin Luther King, too, the religious appeal which paid handsome dividends also demanded its penalties. The conflict with other and more militant black leaders, like Stokely Carmichael and Malcolm X, which troubled Martin in the 1960s, was partly due to their suspicions that at heart he was a revivalist preacher rather than a determined revolutionary. Yet it is a fascinating reflection on the American civil rights scene that even a militant leader like Malcolm X had to resort to a religious appeal – in his case that of the black Muslims – in order to put across his message.

These, then, are common features in the campaigns of Mahatma Gandhi and Martin Luther King: an appeal to an external authority; an appeal to an audience outside the immediate struggle; a careful use of the media; and an appeal to a common religious sentiment.

A Technique for Loving – The Possibilities for Non-Violence

In Chapters 2 and 3 we traced the development of ideas of non-violence in Christian and Indian traditions. In India, different religious influences have contributed to the idea of *ahimsa*, which is an important element in neo-Hinduism and Buddhism. The social practice of Hindu religion, through caste observances, also draws heavily upon some aspects of *ahimsa* in the significance it attaches to vegetarianism. Indian attitudes to *ahimsa* are varied, however, and their ambivalence is increased by the fact that Hinduism is a vast complex of many different beliefs and practices, no one of which can be termed orthodox; and by the pervasiveness in Jaina, Hindu and Buddhist traditions of a notion of renunciation which regards liberation from the delusions and restrictions of the material world to be the highest goal of the religious quest. In Gandhian terms, the opposition of soul-force to body-force is a natural corollary of an emphasis upon such a renunciation, and poses serious problems for the construction of a consistent theory of non-violent resistance. Gandhiji, in drawing upon certain limited aspects of the Christian tradition in formulating his *satyagraha*, was not only providing us with a fascinating example of the value of cross-cultural fertilization, but also remedying a deficiency in his own Gujarati tradition.

The development of Christian attitudes to violence also reveals significant defects in the application of Christian theology to issues of war and peace. Initially, as we have seen, it was assumed that pacifism was the appropriate response to the teaching of Jesus. The first major theological challenge to this came with the adoption of Christianity as the religion of the state. How were Christians to deal with the problems thrust upon them by the responsibilities of power at national and international levels? Theologians responded by justifying the participation of Christians in warfare. Sometimes they simply seemed to be following the dictates of the state and providing theological arguments for what, on other grounds, were regarded as necessities. However, the justification for Christians taking part in war was carefully hedged about by the theories of the just war. Certain sections of the population were to be exempt from the duty to bear arms and safe from the danger of attack. Warfare was not to involve the clergy, or women and children. War was also to be restricted by a ban on fighting in certain seasons and on particular days and by limits placed upon the weapons that could be employed in Christian warfare.

The second challenge was posed during the Crusades, and involved the question of whether or not the rules of the just war should be applied in wars of religion fought against non-Christians. The first compromise, leading to the just war theory, had involved some careful theological sophistry. The response to this second challenge was catastrophic. The New Testament concept of *agape*, a caring, compassionate, sacrificial love extended to friend and foe alike, was set aside in a flood of religious bigotry which accepted a different set of standards and different rules of conduct for warfare against the infidel and the heretic. Nevertheless, the just war was still notionally adhered to among Christian nations, and some standards of civilized, if not entirely Christian, conduct could be appealed to in the conduct of war.

The third challenge is very recent and awaits an appropriate theological response. It is the challenge presented to the just war theory and to the whole question of how, if at all, Christians ought to participate in war, by the advent of modern weapons. The pattern-bombing used in World War Two raised crucial questions of conscience, although until quite recently the full facts upon which a sound judgment could be based were not available. Nuclear weapons have sharpened the questions cruelly. Can Christians now, in good conscience, take any part in war, or in the threat of war implicit in the nuclear deterrent? If not, must they adopt a pacifist stance and contract out of matters relating to the use of power and conflicts between states?

In order to appreciate more fully the force of this third, and contemporary, challenge to a Christian theology of peace, let us consider the implications of recent developments in warfare.

During the 1930s, strategists were aware of the possibilities of aerial bombardment as an instrument of war and of the ethical questions it raised.[1] The Second World War transformed theory into brutal practice, and important moral implications of allied policy were deliberately blurred or concealed from the public.

The first crucial decision, from the point of view of the ethics of war, was that British bombing of Germany should be aimed at civilian rather than military targets with the primary intention of destroying the morale of the civilian population. So Paskins and Dockrill, in their careful study, claim that:

> . . . at the tactical level, the level of air force strategy, the idea of bombing to destroy morale was adopted unequivocally for the first time in the history of human warfare.[2]

This policy was not deliberately made public. Indeed, Sir Archibald Sinclair, Secretary of State for Air, did his best to counter suggestions that bombing was aimed primarily at civilian targets.

> He did not deny that severe and sometimes vast damage was done to residential areas, but he implied or sometimes stated that this was incidental and regrettable. On 28 October 1943 he had explained to Portal that only in this way could he satisfy the enquiries of the Archbishop of Canterbury, the Moderator of the Church of Scotland and other religious leaders since moral condemnation of the bomber offensive by them might disturb the morale of the bomber crews.[3]

The policy adopted by the RAF was partly the result of the great difficulties of bombing with any degree of accuracy over enemy territory at night. This problem was especially acute during the early years of the war.

> A study made in 1941 indicated that of those planes that actually succeeded in attacking their target (about two-thirds of the attacking force) only one-third dropped their bombs within five miles of the point aimed at.[4]

Even with the development of the 'Pathfinder' force of Mosquito fighter-bombers which was intended to increase the accuracy of bombing, it was still possible,

> to make the kind of mistake which once led the Pathfinders to mistake Dobrany for Pilsen and a lunatic asylum for the Skoda works.[5]

But the bombing of civilian housing was not simply the result of inaccuracy. It was deliberate policy. Sir Arthur Harris, of Bomber

Command, said in 1943 that with housing the technically inescapable main target, the destruction of factories could be regarded as a bonus.[6] Lord Cherwell, in 1942, expressed the thought that it should be possible to render one third of the German population homeless by 1943.[7]

The first of the 1000-bomber raids occurred in 1942, having been suggested by Harris and approved by Sir Charles Portal, Chief of the Air Staff, and by Churchill. 1046 bombers dropped 1455 tons of bombs on Cologne, destroying 600 acres of the built-up area of the city.[8] The climax came in mid-February 1945, only three months before the end of the war in Europe, with the attack on Dresden. 800 Lancasters of the RAF attacked Dresden on the night of 13–14 February, causing casualties which were put by German sources at 32,000. The raid was followed by daylight bombing by the US Strategic Air Force, which sent 400 aircraft on the 14th, 200 on the 15th and 400 on the 2nd March.[9]

Even the enthusiasm of Winston Churchill was dampened by this ruthless attack on a civilian population, although his equivocation appears to have been based upon strategic rather than moral considerations. On 28 March 1945 Churchill sent a memorandum to Portal and Lord Ismay in which he wrote:

> It seems to me that the moment has come when the question of the bombing of German cities, simply for the sake of increasing the terror, should be reviewed. Otherwise we shall come into control of an utterly ruined land. We shall not, for instance, be able to get housing materials out of Germany for our own needs because some temporary provision would have to be made for the Germans themselves. The destruction of Dresden remains a serious query against the conduct of Allied bombing. I am of the opinion that military objectives must henceforward be more strictly studied in our interests rather than that of the enemy.
>
> The Foreign Secretary has spoken to me on this subject, and I feel the need for more precise concentration upon military objectives, such as oil and communications behind the immediate battle zone rather than on mere acts of terror and wanton destruction, however impressive.[10]

The acts of terror and wanton destruction were not a marked success in military terms; the supposition that in purely strategic terms war could be pursued most effectively by terrorizing civilian populations was not confirmed by the events of World War Two.[11]

But the consequences for the ethics of war were considerable. It is estimated that,

> As a direct result of a policy of terror bombing by the leaders of Britain, some 200,000 Germans, most of them civilians, were killed and another 780,000 seriously injured.[12]

Mass bombing by the use of conventional weapons raised serious moral questions, but the invention of the atomic bomb made the dreadful figures of destruction at Dresden and Cologne appear paltry by comparison. The first atomic bomb was exploded in the deserts of New Mexico on 16 July 1945. By that time Japan was facing certain defeat but not yet willing to surrender unconditionally. The impression is often given that the allies were then faced with a choice between using the atomic bomb and engaging in bitter island-to-island fighting all the way to Japan at a cost of perhaps a million American lives. This is the way President Truman presented the choice he claimed faced him when he had to decide whether or not to authorize the use of the atomic bomb. It was an understanding supported by the US Army, which feared the casualties which might ensue from further land fighting. But there do appear to have been other alternatives.

The US Navy and Air Force are known to have advocated the use of a naval blockade or a strategic air offensive. But either of those policies would have taken time, and time introduced another factor. The Soviet Union was on the point of declaring war on Japan, and Russian participation in the war would have led to Russian claims for a share in the spoils of victory. Was it the case, as some historians have suggested, that a desire to keep Russia out of the Japanese conflict was an important factor in deciding to use the bomb?[13]

In addition to the possibilities of blockade or air offensive there was open to the Allies the possibility of pursuing a negotiated peace with Japan.

> Japan was known to have been putting out official peace feelers in May and June 1945 and 12 July (four days before the first atom bomb test) the US intercepted a message from the Japanese Foreign Minister to the Japanese ambassador in Moscow.[14]

The message instructed the ambassador to make clear the Japanese desire to find an end to the war, and to say that the only obstacle to an immediate peace was the Allied demand for unconditional surrender.

Yet another alternative to the use of the atomic bomb on Hiroshima and Nagasaki was to provide a non-military demonstration of the bomb. This course of action was actually suggested by nuclear scientists working in the United States.

So it was in spite of the availability of alternatives rather than because of their lack that the decision was taken by President Truman to use the atomic bomb. Even then, the choice of target could have provided yet another option. Robert Batchelder suggested:

> Had the target been a supply dump of equipment essential to the defense of the Kyushi invasion beaches, the impact upon General Anami and his friends (who favoured a last-ditch stand against the US) might have been greater than was that of the destruction of Hiroshima.[15]

The first bomb was dropped on Hiroshima on 6 August 1945. The Japanese did not surrender. The generals attempted to minimize reports of the damage and were not immediately persuaded of the need to surrender by the fearful injuries imposed upon the civilian population. US planning had suggested 11 August as the date for the second bomb, should it prove necessary. Weather reports indicated that 11 August would not be suitable, and one might have expected that the dropping of the second bomb would have been delayed. In fact the bombing of Nagasaki was brought forward from the 11 to the 9 August. The only factor that appears to account for this curious haste in dropping the second bomb was the entry of Russia into the war against Japan on August 8.

After the Nagasaki bombing a divided Japanese Cabinet was persuaded by the Emperor to accept surrender. In doing so they insisted that the surrender should not 'prejudice the prerogatives of His Majesty as a Sovereign Ruler'.[16] Thus unconditional surrender was offered with a condition which the allies accepted. Might they not have negotiated such a surrender without the use of the atomic bombs? Michael Walzer's comment seems to be well justified:

> In the summer of 1945 the victorious Americans owed the Japanese people an experiment in negotiation. To use the atomic bomb, to kill and terrorize civilians, without even attempting such an experiment, was a double crime.[17]

The bombings of Hiroshima and Nagasaki were unsavoury incidents. The decison to use the bombs did not rest upon such clear-cut choices as official records of the war have suggested. The use of the atomic bombs well illustrates the difficulties of making rational and moral decisions in wartime, when emotions are heated, information deliberately distorted by governments or factions within governments, and politicians often manipulated by powerful military leaders. But the acquiescence by Western governments in the use of atomic weapons against Japan, together with their acceptance of area bombing in the European war, indicates the extent to which the guiding principles of the just war theory had fallen into disuse even within nations professedly Christian, whose public pronouncements made much of the need to defend Christian civilization.

Of course, I accept that in the Second World War the Allies were engaged in a bitter struggle against ruthless opponents who themselves did many terrible things. But to condemn the atrocities of the Nazis in the concentration camps or the Japanese guards in prisoner-of-war camps is not to excuse action taken by the Allies against civilian populations, especially when such action as area or atomic bombing was of limited strategic value and when there were alternatives available. There is an impressive weight of opinion among academics which supports the view that bombing tactics employed in World War Two infringed the conventions of behaviour in war ostensibly accepted by the Allies. So, for example, Michael Walzer:

> . . . the rule against the deliberate killing of civilians (non-combatants) in wartime is very old and its moral value widely recognized. Its application to the problems of aerial bombardment was, in 1940, fairly recent, not yet incorporated in international treaties and conventions, but there could be no doubt as to the practical requirements of the rule, broadly understood.[18]

More forcefully, Paskins and Dockrill claim that the Allied bombing campaign,

> could have been brought to trial under inter-war legislation. It violated fundamental moral principles. It is often mentioned in criticism of Nuremberg, as a leading example of double standards.[19]

Most notably, perhaps, the Oxford moral philosopher G. E. M. Anscombe has vigorously defended the principle of the immunity of non-combatants, a principle which she asserts was infringed by the area bombing of German cities and the dropping of the atomic bombs. Miss Anscombe led opposition to the proposal of Oxford

University to award an honorary degree to Mr Truman in 1958 on the grounds that the bombing of Hiroshima and Nagasaki was an act of mass murder.[20]

Michael Walzer suggests that even the British Government tacitly admitted how dubious its policy of area bombing had been by not honouring Sir Arthur Harris or Bomber Command after the War.[21]

The failure of conventional moral standards to influence policy in the Second World War has serious implications, not least because the defence strategy of the West since 1945 has relied upon the fearsome threat of the nuclear deterrent. The use of nuclear weapons infringes Christian moral theory even more clearly than did area bombing or the atomic bombs. But deterrence itself is open to equally serious moral objections.

> It is as if the state should seek to prevent murder by threatening to kill the family and friends of every murderer – a domestic version of the policy of 'massive retaliation'. Surely that would be a repugnant policy. We would not admire the police officials who designed it or those pledged to carry it out, even if they never actually killed anybody. I don't want to say that such people would necessarily be transformed into barbarians; they might well have a heightened sense of how awful murder is and a heightened desire to avoid it; they might loathe the work they were pledged to do and fervently hope that they never had to do it. Nevertheless, the enterprise is immoral. The immorality lies in the threat itself, not in its present or even its likely consequences.[22]

The objections to the actual use of nuclear weapons are clear enough, from the background of the just war. Nuclear war involves attacking civilian targets, and so infringes the demand to distinguish between combatants and non-combatants. To this problem, already inherent in area bombing, is added the difficulty of winning a nuclear war ('moral certainty that the side of justice will emerge victorious'). The theory of nuclear defence assumes an act of retaliation after one's own state has been crippled or destroyed, which clearly infringes the notion of proportionality, and accepts the impossibility of defending a civilian population. Even the notion that war is permissible in order to preserve the integrity of the state is called into question by nuclear war. An all-out nuclear war would lead to the destruction of nation states as we now know them. As Paskins and Dockrill point out, those who argue that nuclear wars can be fought and won, do so within a context of orthodox political theory which takes for granted the pursuit of the self-interest of the State. It is absurd to attempt to justify nuclear war in terms of protecting the integrity of a state if in the process of waging such war the state itself is likely to be destroyed. 'The political rationale for seeking to survive a nuclear war is deeply obscure.'[23]

Those who pursue this obscure policy are also playing with enormous risks. A former Kennedy White House staff member recently commented that the development of ever more accurate nuclear weapons and the means of delivering them to their targets 'makes the military environment far less stable today than it has ever been'.[24]

The policy of deterrence, then, is open to very serious objections. As long ago as 1961 a World Council of Churches Report declared:

> Christians have no alternative but openly to declare that the all-out use of these weapons (nuclear weapons) should never be resorted to.[25]

A report commissioned by the United Reformed Church and published in 1973 stated more cautiously:

> . . . there is increasing doubt whether modern war can ever comply with the traditional canons of the 'just' war.[26]

There are, to be sure, Christian theologians who have attempted to justify nuclear warfare, and especially the use of tactical nuclear weapons against opposing armies rather than against cities. Paul Ramsey argues for this position, and suggests that something he calls the 'collateral civilian damage' in such warfare (that is, the civilians who are not primary targets but are killed incidentally) would be morally acceptable and yet would be sufficient to act as a deterrent.[27] His argument seems to me to be unconvincing when measured against the values implicit in the just war theory. But more important is the fact that Ramsey is attempting to state a position which is neither all-out nuclear war nor pacifism. There is, I believe, a better alternative.

The moral as well as the technical arguments relating to modern warfare are necessarily very complex. What seems to me to be beyond dispute is that the carefully thought-out notions of limited warfare, restricted to certain sections of the population and having regard to the immunity of non-combatants, fought with limited weapons in defence of territorial integrity and of justice – the just war theory – cannot apply to nuclear war or to large-scale pattern bombing of civilian targets.

An additional point deserves mention here, partly because it played a significant part in Martin Luther King's objections to the Vietnam War. That is the matter of the cost of modern defence spending, when measured against other and more humanitarian uses of scarce resources. Martin King recognized that the Vietnam War was diverting public money which was essential if programmes to improve the position of the Negro in American society were to be implemented with any degree of seriousness. Christian theology today also has to take some account of the vast sums of money required to maintain the nuclear deterrent, and the consequent lack of funds available for more useful enterprises, including development in the poorer countries of the world. It would be tedious to make a long list of comparative expenditure on arms and aid. Two simple examples must be sufficient. The first is that the equivalent of an entire year's budget for the United Nations and all its specialized agencies is spent around the world on arms every two days. The second is that the cost of one Trident submarine is equal to the cost of a year's schooling for sixteen million children in developing countries.[28] Many more such sums could be provided, but the point is a simple one. The cost of a deterrent policy is enormous even for the richest countries in the world; for the not-so-rich it is crippling.

It is also a curious feature of deterrent policy that its proponents assume the necessity of the accumulation of ever greater stocks of weapons, even when there is no possibility of their being used. So ten years ago the nuclear weapons stockpiled in the USA and the Soviet Union had reached the explosive equivalent of 5.15 tons of TNT for every man, woman and child on earth. The USA has sufficient nuclear armoury to obliterate every Russian city of over 100,000 people, not once, but forty times.[29] The prodigality of such defence spending is at the expense of more laudable projects.

An assessment of the acknowledged immorality of mass-bombing and nuclear war, and of the serious moral problems involved in the whole theory of nuclear deterrence, leads to one inescapable conclusion. That is that the just war theory can no longer be applied. It would appear that Christians (and indeed all who take seriously the moral ideas implicit in the notion of the just war) can no longer in good conscience take part in war or in the threat of war implicit in the nuclear deterrent. Is the alternative, then, simply one of absolute pacifism, a contracting out of matters relating to the use of power and to conflicts between states?

Mahatma Gandhi and Martin Luther King Jr, in their fascinating mixing of Christian and Indian traditions, point the way towards an answer to this perplexing question.

Gandhi evolved a technique of non-violent resistance out of a variety of ideas and experiences. His approach to conflict was positive and his opposition to injustice vigorous. He was deeply conscious of the importance of moral constraints in informing judgments about practical political issues, and concerned to relate means and ends. His own thought was richly embued with religious ideas culled from different traditions, but all relating to what seemed to him to be the central religious idea of renunciation. Yet for all his emphasis upon renunciation Mahatma Gandhi was not an absolute pacifist. The Satyagraha he developed was an active and positive method for opposing tyranny which expressed very clearly his strong commitment to non-violence and his belief that truth and goodness must in the end prevail over falsehood and evil.

We have seen how Martin Luther King adapted Mahatma Gandhi's techniques to the situation of the civil rights movement. Gandhianism provided a method of action which effectively expressed the peculiarly Christian concept of *agape*, an understanding of love which to Martin King was the foundation of Christian moral practice. Taking Gandhianism out of its Indian context enabled Martin Luther King to dispense with the elements of celibacy, vegetarianism, and a renunciation which opposed body-force with soul-force. Martin Luther King was concerned to seize and use power, but in its pursuit he was dedicated to non-violence. In its cause he opposed the pressing claims of black power, and for its sake he accepted criticism and sometimes abuse from radical blacks. Yet I have argued that, like Gandhi, Martin Luther King was never quite absolutely pacifist. For most of his all-too-short public life he was caught up in the civil rights movement, and his thinking about non-violence was related to that. During the last few years of his life he turned his attention to the Vietnam War and opposed that completely. But he had not had the opportunity to formulate a comprehensive and consistent set of attitudes to questions of peace and war.

A concern for the distinction between *satyagraha* and pacifism may appear to be pedantic. But given the current situation, in which acquiescence to national policy on war involves acceptance of the possibility of nuclear bombardment and so inevitably a rejection of what is meant by the just war, and in which the alternative of complete pacifism appears to be simply surrender, the distinction is of considerable importance.

Non-violent resistance which is not quite pacifism, but is nevertheless informed by the examples of Gandhi and King, appears to offer a real alternative to all-out war on the one hand and pacific inertia on the other. A carefully thought-out programme of non-violent resistance offers to the person of conscience a way out of the paralysis engendered by what appears to be an impossible choice between obviously immoral mass warfare and ineffective pacifism.

What might such a programme involve? In dealing with questions of peace, war, and non-violent resistance the theologian is concerned to state principles which should inform the actions of politicians and military strategists and to point out the consequences for religion and morality of the choices that might be made. It is the task of the strategist to work out in detail a programme of non-violent resistance. But it would be cowardly to leave the discussion at this point without making some specific suggestions, in very general terms, of how I see the possibility of non-violent resistance being applied to the current situation in my own country. In making such suggestions I am emboldened by the fact that it is not military strategists or soldiers who have established the creative models of non-violent resistance but the religio-political figures of Mahatma Gandhi and Martin Luther King Jr.

The application of a policy of non-violent resistance to Britain's situation would involve first the recognition that we should not engage in mass bombing, nuclear war, or other deliberate and terrorizing attacks on non-combatants.

Secondly, and as a consequence, the nation would cease to rely on the nuclear deterrent. One result of this would be to remove the great threat which results from the siting of American missiles in this country. At the moment a potential enemy of the USA must regard Britain as a primary target. A conflict, perhaps even a threatened conflict or the fear of an American attack, would necessitate the potential enemy attacking Britain, with obviously disastrous consequences for our small and heavily populated island. The first result of ceasing to rely on the nuclear deterrent may well be to increase our safety immeasurably.

Thirdly, it becomes necessary to turn to the question of what kind of defence might be appropriate if these first two points are implemented. And here the distinction between pacifism and non-violent resistance becomes crucial. Pacifism as an absolute principle leads to all kinds of difficulties which are rehearsed at length in books on the morality of war. What, for example, is the pacifist to do if his family is attacked? Does he, on the basis of his pacifist principles, simply stand by and watch? How does the absolute pacifist deal with problems to do with policing, and the degree of force necessary to accomplish effective civil control? What is the attitude of the absolute pacifist to international peace-keeping forces which for all their peaceful intentions are nevertheless armed forces composed of soldiers ready to use their weapons? To what extent can a pacifist logically take part in national politics if his party or his country do not share his convictions? (George Lansbury, in the 1930s, was adjured by Ernest Bevin to stop hawking his conscience around from conference to conference. As a pacifist, it was implied, he was incapable of offering realistic leadership to the Labour Party.) These questions are not incapable of being answered, after a fashion. But the pure pacifist almost inevitably becomes embroiled in them, and pacifism as a refusal of all participation in warfare comes to be regarded as simply impractical.

That is why it matters that non-violent resistance as expounded by Mahatma Gandhi and Martin Luther King does not necessarily involve pacifism. It is equally consistent with the attitude described in Chapter 10 as pacificism. Non-violent resistance can be employed as a dominant theory of defence without necessarily ruling out the use of physical force against an enemy in certain circumstances.

Non-violent resistance as a form of defence against an aggressor depends largely upon the difficulty of governing a modern industrial country without the consent of the governed. A programme of non-violent resistance necessarily concedes the likelihood of the country being overrun. It does not have the means to directly confront and halt an enemy invasion. What it does attempt to do is to make the task of governing so difficult that ultimately it is not worth the effort.

The methods of a programme of non-violent resistance would include those used in the campaigns of Gandhi and Martin Luther King: the methods of boycott, strike, civil disobedience and non-cooperation. Gandhi and King both came to appreciate the necessity of training non-violent resisters in their difficult task. Training of people on a large scale and over an appreciable period of time would be a necessary pre-condition of an effective programme of non-violent resistance. The resources to do this could very easily be provided once the country had withdrawn its enormously expensive programme of nuclear armament. Some specific proposals for training in non-violent resistance were made by the United Reformed Church in 1973, and included the suggestions that the armed forces should be trained in techniques of non-violent resistance, that special forces of civilians should be trained for non-violent peacekeeping operations, and that churches should sponsor non-violent training schools for political activists.[30]

The consequences of training a large number of people over a long period should not be under-estimated. Michael Walzer comments on the fact that no non-violent struggle has yet been undertaken by a people trained in advance in its methods and prepared as soldiers are in time of war to accept its costs.[31]

An enemy wishing to occupy the country would have to weigh the political or territorial advantages they saw accruing from an occupation against the costs. The economic cost of occupation would be high. A large number of troops would be needed for policing purposes. But in addition to that, the enemy power would have to bring in its own personnel to run a civilian government and possibly also to provide the essential services of power, transport, and whatever else it deemed necessary to keep the country manageable and productive. The political cost would also be high. There is plenty of evidence from the post-war period of the difficulty of maintaining morale among soldiers who have to perform the unpleasant tasks of an army of occupation living among an unfriendly people. In such a situation it could be expected that the soldiers'

> military elan might well fade, their morale erode, under the strains of civilian hostility and of an ongoing struggle in which they never experienced the release of an open fight.[32]

The policy of determined non-violent resistance would be known to a potential aggressor in advance, and an enemy would then have to take account of the long-term economic, political, and military problems that would be created by an invasion. Of course, suffering and casualties among the invaded people would be inevitable; but it is difficult to envisage any situation of civil resistance which would result in the number of deaths, the extent of injuries, and the destruction of society which would follow a nuclear confrontation.

It must be acknowledged that as with any other conceivable defence policy, a policy of civil resistance presents problems. In examining the tactics of Mahatma Gandhi and Martin Luther King we noticed some common features of their more successful campaigns.[33] Both were able on occasion to appeal to some kind of external authority, be it a distant British parliament or a federal government. The possibility of appealing to an external authority cannot be assumed in a programme of civil resistance, although the influence of the United Nations should not be entirely discounted. Gandhi and King were also able to appeal to a friendly audience outside the immediate struggle, and although a sympathetic audience outside the country may not be hard to come by, the possibility of such an audience doing anything to help is remote.

Mahatma Gandhi and Martin Luther King also had in common their careful use of newspapers and the media to encourage and instruct their supporters and to make their causes known to a wider audience. A programme of non-violent resistance would have to expect to be confronted by a power which exercised total control over communications, and would therefore have to resort to clandestine means for communications among its own supporters. Paskins and Dockrill, anticipating the objection that the utility of non-violence is very restricted, acknowledge that 'superior fire-power can always overcome mere publicity'.[34]

But the circumstances of the campaigns led by Martin King and Gandhi were very different from those envisaged in a situation of invasion, and the tactics they employed were carefully and directly related to the actual problems and possibilities of their own situations. In the case of invasion and occupation by an enemy power, it is possible to envisage a resistance in which the dominant method is non-violent but which does not rule out the use of physical force in certain circumstances. The ideals which undergirded Gandhiji's belief in the value of non-violence were not seen by him to be incompatible with a resort to force in some circumstances. The policy which I am advocating is not one of pure pacifism, but one which would use a technique of non-violent resistance, based upon both principle and its tactical value. The policy would not become embroiled in the pacifist problems which arise from a refusal to use force in any circumstances. The enemy invader would be faced by a well-organized, carefully prepared programme of civil disobedience based upon non-violent action, but he could not rest secure in the knowledge that among the conquered people there would never be recourse to violence aimed at carefully selected targets for specific purposes. A combination of a massive policy of non-violent resistance, using large numbers of people well-trained in advance, together with some strictly limited and carefully controlled military action, may well make occupation an unpleasant and ultimately undesirable choice for an invader. Paskins and Dockrill, who candidly acknowledge the problems of using civil disobedience in totalitarian states, also point out that,

> . . . very little appears to be known about the possibility of combining massive non-violent action with such practices as clandestine leadership and selective assassination.[35]

The post-Second World War period has provided many examples of the ability of small groups with strictly limited military resources avoiding major military encounters and relying upon a warfare of evasion. A combination of strictly limited military action with a large-scale programme of non-violent resistance offers a resolution of the dilemma created by the apparent need to choose between all-out nuclear warfare and pacifism.

The fourth factor identified as common to the campaigns of Mahatma Gandhi and Martin Luther King was the appeal both men made, in very different ways, to a religious constituency. In present-day Britain the common ideological base of an appeal to non-violence is more likely to rest upon moral rather than strictly religious convictions. But the fact that this study has shown how two markedly different religious traditions have contributed to each other in the formation of *satyagraha* augurs well for the possibility of finding a widely acceptable basis for non-violent resistance in multi-cultural Britain.

The possibilities of non-violent resistance are great, and still largely unexplored. In perilous times we would do well to heed the teaching and example of Mahatma Gandhi and the adaptation of his work by Martin Luther King Jr. They have given the world remarkable demonstrations of a technique for loving; a technique which resolutely seeks justice, but also desires only good for those against whom the struggle is carried out and works for the ultimate benefit of friend and foe alike; a technique which speaks in the positive phrases of co-operation rather than the negative tones of confrontation; a technique which demands of its users much courage, tenacity and sensitivity; and a technique which blends in an unusually effective way moral and spiritual insights from East and West.

Bibliography

Aurobindo, Sri, *The Doctrine of Passive Resistance*, Arya Publishing House, Calcutta 1948

Bainton, R. H., *Christian Attitudes Toward War and Peace*, Hodder and Stoughton 1961

Bapat, P. V. (ed.), *2500 Years of Buddhism*, Government of India 1956

Bary, W. T. de (ed.), *Sources of Indian Tradition* (two vols), Columbia University Press 1958

Basham, A. L., *A Cultural History of India*, Clarendon Press 1975

Bhagavad Gita, The, Tapovanam Publishing House, Tirupparaitturai 1965

Bhargava, D., *Jaina Ethics*, Motilal Banarsidas, Delhi 1968

Bishop, P. D., 'Ahimsa and Satyagraha: the Interaction of Hindu and Christian Religious Ideas and their contribution to a Political Campaign', *Indian Journal of Theology* 27, 2, 1978

—, *Words in World Religions*, SCM Press 1979

Bondurant, J. V., *Conquest of Violence – the Gandhian Philosophy of Conflict*, Oxford University Press, Bombay 1959

Booth, K., and Wright, M. (eds.), *American Thinking about Peace and War*, Harvester Press 1978

Brandon, S. G. F., *Jesus and the Zealots*, Manchester University Press 1967

—, *The Trial of Jesus*, Batsford and Stein and Day, New York 1968

Brandt, R. B., et al. (ed.), *War and Moral Responsibility*, Princeton University Press 1974

Brecher, M., *Nehru – A Political Biography*, Oxford University Press 1959

Brown, Judith M., *Gandhi's Rise to Power – Indian Politics 1915–1922*, Cambridge University Press 1972

—, *Gandhi and Civil Disobedience*, Cambridge University Press 1977

Butterfield, H., *Christianity, Diplomacy and War*, Epworth Press 1962

—, *Christianity and History*, Fontana Books 1957

Carter, A., Hogget, D., and Roberts, A., *Non-Violent Action: A Selected Bibliography*, Housmans 1970

Ceadel, M., *Pacifism in Britain 1914–1945. The Defining of a Faith*, Oxford University Press 1980

Cousins, N. (ed.), *Profiles of Gandhi*, Indian Book Co., Delhi 1969

Davies, J. G., *Christians, Politics and Violent Revolution*, SCM Press 1976

Devanesen, C., *The Making of the Mahatma*, Orient Longmans 1969

Diwakar, R. R., *Satyagraha: Its Techniques and History*, Hind Kitabs, Bombay 1946

—, *Satyagraha in Action*, Signet Press, Calcutta 1949

Duncan, R. (ed.), *Selected Writings of Mahatma Gandhi*, Fontana Books 1972

Edwards, M., *Nehru – A Political Biography*, Collins 1969

Ferguson, J., *The Politics of Love*, James Clarke 1972

—, *War and Peace in the World's Religions*, Sheldon Press 1977

Fischer, E., and Jain, J., *Art and Ritual – 2500 Years of Jainism in India*, Sterling Publications, New Delhi 1977

Gandhi, M. K., *The Collected Works of Mahatma Gandhi (CWMG)*, Government of India 1958–1976 (sixty-seven volumes: an exhaustive collection of Gandhi's words, including speeches, letters and interviews)

—, *Gita – My Mother*, Pearl Pubs Private Ltd, Bombay 1965

—, *An Autobiography, or The Story of My Experiment With Truth*, Ahmedabad, 1927 and 1929 (see Narayan, S. (ed.), *The Selected Works*)

—, *Non-Violence in Peace and War*, Ahmedabad, Vol. 1, 1942; Vol. 2, 1949

Garrow, D. J., *Protest at Selma – Martin Luther King Jr and the Voting Rights Acts of 1965*, Yale University Press 1978

Gopal, S. (ed.), *Selected Works of Jawaharlal Nehru*, Orient Longman 1972 (eight volumes)

Gopalan, S., *Outlines of Jainism*, Wiley Eastern Private Ltd, New Delhi 1973

Gregg, R. B., *The Psychology and Strategy of Gandhi's Non-Violent Resistance*, S. Ganesan, Madras 1929

Griffiths, P., *Modern India*, Ernest Benn [4]1965

Glick, W., (ed.), *Henry D. Thoreau; Reform Papers*, Princeton University Press 1973

Hardy, P., *The Muslims of British India*, Cambridge University Press 1972

Hare, A. P., and Blumberg, H., *Nonviolent Direct Action*, Corpus Books 1968

Harvey, J. C., *Black Civil Rights During the Johnson Administration*, University and College Press, Mississippi 1973

Horsburgh, H. J. N., *Non-Violence and Aggression – A Study of Gandhi's Moral Equivalent to War*, Oxford University Press 1968

Huie, W. B., *He Slew the Dreamer*, W. H. Allen 1970

Huttenback, R. A., *Gandhi in South Africa – British Imperialism and the Indian Question 1860–1914*, Cornell University Press 1971

Indian National Congress, *Punjab Disturbances 1919–1920* (two vols, first published 1920), Deep Publications, New Delhi 1976

Iyer, R., *The Moral and Political Thought of Mahatma Gandhi*, Oxford University Press 1973

Jaini, J., *Outlines of Jainism*, Cambridge University Press 1916

King, Coretta S., *My Life With Martin Luther King Jr*, Hodder and Stoughton 1970

King, Martin Luther, Jr, *Stride Toward Freedom*, Gollancz 1959

—, *Strength to Love*, Harper and Row, New York 1963, and Hodder and Stoughton 1964

—, *Why We Can't Wait*, Harper and Row, New York 1964

—, *Chaos or Community?* Hodder and Stoughton 1967

—, *Trumpet of Conscience*, Hodder and Stoughton 1968

King-Hall, S., *Defence in the Nuclear Age*, Gollancz 1958

Kotturan, G., *Ahimsa. Gautama to Gandhi*, Sterling Publications Private Ltd, New Delhi 1973

Kripalani, J. B., *Non-Violent Revolution*, Vora, Bombay 1938

Lewis, D. L., *Martin Luther King: A Critical Biography*, Allen Lane: The Penguin Press 1970

Ling, T., *The Buddha*, Penguin Books 1976

—, *Buddhism, Imperialism and War*, Allen and Unwin 1979

-, *Buddhist Revival in India*, Macmillan 1980

MacGregor, G. H. C., *The New Testament Basis of Pacifism*, Fellowship of Reconciliation, London 1958 (revised edition)

Macquarrie, J., *The Concept of Peace*, SCM Press 1973

Mahadevan, T. K. (ed.), *Civilian Defence*, Gandhi Peace Foundation, New Delhi 1967

Majumdar, R. C., Raychaudari, H. C., and Datta, K., *An Advanced History of India*, Macmillan 1965

Marshall, I. H., *The Gospel of Luke*, Paternoster Press 1978

Martin, Britan, *New India, 1885*, University of California Press 1969

Martin, D. A., *Pacifism – An Historical and Sociological Study*, Routledge and Kegan Paul 1965

Maurice, M. S., *The Ethics of Passive Resistance*, Ganesh, Madras

Mayer, P. (ed.), *The Pacifist Conscience*, Penguin Books 1966

Mehta, V., *Mahatma Gandhi and His Apostles*, Andre Deutsch 1977

Meltzer, M., *Thoreau: People, Principles and Politics*, Hill and Wang, New York 1963

Miller, W. R., *Non-Violence: A Christian Interpretation*, Allen and Unwin 1964

—, *Martin Luther King Jr: His Life, Martyrdom and Meaning for the World*, Weybright and Talley, New York 1968

Minz, N., *Mahatma Gandhi and Hindu-Christian Dialogue*, CLS, Madras 1970

Moore, R. J., *Liberalism and Indian Politics, 1872–1922*, Edward Arnold 1966

Morris, C., *Unyoung, Uncoloured, Unpoor*, Epworth Press 1969

Murthi, V. V. R., *Non-Violence in Politics: A Study of Gandhian Techniques and Thinking*, Frank Bros, Delhi 1958

Nanda, B. R., *Mahatma Gandhi*, Allen and Unwin 1965 (revised edition)

Narayan, S. (ed.), *The Selected Works of Mahatma Gandhi (SWME)*, Navajivan Publishing House, Ahmedabad 1968 (six volumes)
  Vols. 1 and 2, *An Autobiography, or The Story of My Experiments With Truth*, first published, Vol. 1, 1927; Vol. 2, 1929
  Vol. 3 *Satyagraha in South Africa*, first English edition 1928
  Vol. 4 *The Basic Works* (pamphlets and brochures from 1907 onwards)
  Vol. 5 *Selected Letters*
  Vol. 6 *The Voice of Truth* (a selection of speeches)

Nehru, J., *India's Freedom*, Allen and Unwin 1962

Niebuhr, Reinhold, *Moral Man and Immoral Society*, Scribner, New York 1932 and SCM Press 1963

—, *The Nature and Destiny of Man*, Scribners, New York and Nisbet 1941–43

Nikhilananda, *Hinduism*, Allen and Unwin 1958

O'Dwyer, M., *India as I Knew It*, Constable 1925

Olson, T., and Shivers, L., *Training for Non-Violent Action*, Friends Peace and International Relations Committee, London 1970

Pandy, B. N., *The Break-Up of British India*, Macmillan 1969

Paris, P., *Black Leaders in Conflict*, Pilgrim Press, New York 1978

Paskins, B., and Dockrill, M., *The Ethics of War*, Duckworth 1979

Pocock, D., *Mind, Body and Wealth*, Blackwell 1973

Rawlinson, H. G., *India – A Short Cultural History* (1937), The Cresset Press 1954

Ramachandran, J., and Mahadevan, T. K., *Non-Violence after Gandhi: A Study of Martin Luther King Jr*, Gandhi Peace Foundation, Delhi 1968

Ramsey, P., *The Just War: Force and Political Responsibility*, Scribner, New York 1968

Robinson, F., *Separatism Among Indian Muslims: Politics of the United Provinces, 1860–1923*, Cambridge University Press 1975

Rockman, J. (ed.), *Peace in Search of Makers*, Judson Press, Valley Forge 1978

Rudolph, L. I. and S. H., *The Modernity of Tradition: Political Development in India*, University of Chicago Press 1970

Ruether, Rosemary R., *Faith and Fratricide: The Theological Roots of Anti-Semitism*, Seabury Press, New York 1974

Russell, F. H., *The Just War in the Middle Ages*, Cambridge University Press 1975

Sadhatissa, H., *Buddhist Ethics*, Allen and Unwin 1970

Sangharakshita, *The Three Jewels*, Rider 1967

Schulke, F. (ed.), *Martin Luther King Jr. A Documentary . . . Montgomery to Memphis*, Norton, New York 1976

Shridarani, K., *War Without Violence*, New York 1939

Singh, K. N., *Gandhi and Marx: An Ethico-Philosophical Study*, Associated Book Agency, Patna 1979

Spear, P., *The Oxford History of Modern India*, Oxford University Press (India) 1974

Stein, W., *Nuclear Weapons and Christian Conscience*, Merlin Press nd.

Takulia, H. B., 'The Negro's Experiments with Non-Violent Protest', *Gandhi, Theory and Practice*, Indian Institute of Advanced Study, Simla 1969

Taylor, A. J. P., *The Trouble Makers*, Panther Books 1969

Thomas, M. M., 'Basic Approaches to Power – Gandhiji, Andrews and King', *Religion and Society* XVI, 3, Bangalore 1969

Tolstoy, L., *The Law of Love and the Law of Violence*, Randolph Field, New York 1948

—, *A Confession and What I Believe*, Oxford University Press 1921

—, *The Kingdom of God is Within You*, Heinemann 1894

United Reformed Church, *Non-Violent Action*, SCM Press 1973

US Commission on Civil Rights, *The Voting Rights Act: Ten Years After*, 1975

Vasto, Lanza del, *Gandhi to Vinoba*, Rider 1956

Walzer, M., *Just and Unjust Wars*, Allen Lane: The Penguin Press 1978

Watson, F., and Tennyson, H., *Talking of Gandhi*, BBC Publications 1969

Weber, M., *The Religion of India*, Allen and Unwin 1958 and Free Press, New York 1967

Wilkinson, T. S., and Thomas, M. M., *Ambedkar and the Neo-Buddhist Movement*, CLS Madras 1972

Winter, P., *On the Trial of Jesus*, de Gruyter, Berlin 1961

Wolfenstein, E. V., *The Revolutionary Personality: Lenin, Trotsky, Gandhi*, Princeton University Press 1967

Woodcock, J. H., *Gandhi*, Fontana Books 1972

Woods, J. H., *The Yoga System of Patanjali*, Harvard Oriental Series, Vol. 17, reprinted Motilal Banarsides, Delhi 1966

Zahn, G. C., *War, Conscience and Dissent*, Geoffrey Chapman 1967

I am also indebted to the following periodicals and archive material: *Harijan*, *Young India*, *Times of India*, *Hindustan Times*, Jawaharlal Nehru Papers and Motilal Papers from the collections in the Nehru Memorial Museum and Library, New Delhi, and the N. K. Bose Papers, V. S. S. Sastri Papers and Home Political File from the National Archives of India, New Delhi. Cf. also Stuart Nelson, 'The Gandhian Concept of Non-Violence', Seminar on Non-Violence and Social Change, University of Allahabad 1971, and 'Liberation and Revolution: Gandhi's Challenge', Thirteenth Triennial Conference of War Resisters International, Haverford College, Pennsylvania 1969.

While I was in America in 1980 I had interviews as follows: Revd Dr Eugene Carson Blake, Stamford, Connecticut, 26 July; Revd Ed Brown, Atlanta, 13 August; Dr Cain Felder, Princeton Theological Seminary, 25 July; George Houser, American Committee on Africa, New York 15 August; Revd Albert E. Love, Southern Christian Leadership Conference, Atlanta, 14 August; Revd Martin Luther King, Sr, Atlanta, 7 August; Dr Harold DeWolf, Lakeland, Florida, 29 July.

Notes

Chapter 2　Christian Attitudes to Violence

1. See Josh. 3.9f.: 8.1; 10.7–11.
2. Josh. 6.17,21; 8.25–29.
3. Commemorated in Chanukkah, the beautiful Jewish festival of light which falls in December every year, and recalls the victory of Judas Maccabaeus over Antiochus in 165 BC.
4. See S. G. F. Brandon, *Jesus and the Zealots*, Manchester University Press 1967.
5. Mark 3.18; Luke 6.15.
6. The derivation of Iscariot from *sicarius* is supported by Wellhausen, F. Schulthess, and Cullmann. See I. Howard Marshall, *The Gospel of Luke*, Paternoster Press 1978, pp.239f.
7. Paul Winter, *On the Trial of Jesus*, Walter de Gruyter 1961; S. G. F. Brandon, *The Trial of Jesus*, Batsford 1968; Rosemary Ruether, *Faith and Fratricide: The Theological Roots of Anti-Semitism*, Seabury Press 1974.
8. Colin Morris, *Unyoung, Uncoloured, Unpoor*, Epworth Press 1969.
9. Mark 8.31 RSV.
10. Matthew 5.38–46 RSV.
11. Luke 12.7 RSV.
12. Matthew 5.30 RSV.
13. Romans 12.16,21 NEB.
14. This aspect of the teaching of the New Testament is well summarized by G. H. C. MacGregor, *The New Testament Basis of Pacifism*, Fellowship of Reconciliation 1958, pp.11f.: 'The first principle of Jesus' ethic is love towards one's neighbour. This ethic is in turn based upon belief in a Father God who loves all men impartially and sets an infinite value on every individual human soul. All the teaching of Jesus must be interpreted in the light of his own way of life, and above all of the Cross by which his teaching was sealed.'
15. Romans 13.1 NEB.
16. R. Bainton, *Christian Attitudes Toward War and Peace*, Hodder and Stoughton 1961, p.67: 'From the end of the New Testament period

to the decade AD 170–180, there is no evidence whatever of Christians in the army . . . The reason may have been either that participation was assumed or that abstention was taken for granted. The latter is more probable.'

17. Tertullian, *De Idolatria* XIX, quoted by Bainton, op. cit., p.73.

18. Bainton, op. cit., p.68.

19. Justin Martyr, *Dialogue with Trypho* CX, quoted by Bainton, op. cit., p.72.

20. Quoted ibid, p.79.

21. Ibid., p.73: 'Thus of all the outstanding writers of the East and the West repudiated participation in warfare for Christians.'

22. Cf. F. H. Russell, *The Just War in the Middle Ages*, Cambridge University Press 1975: 'Before Constantine's conversion churchmen tended to condemn warfare in general and Roman wars in particular. On New Testament grounds they concluded that wars violated Christian charity and that Roman wars only resulted in violence and bloodshed. Even while employing military metaphors to describe proper Christian conduct, many Christians rejected worldly military service in favour of the *militia Christi*, a pacific expression of their struggle against evil.'

23. Bainton, op. cit., p.88.

24. Russell, op. cit., p.12.

25. Ibid., p.13.

26. Augustine went even further than justifying participation in a *just* war: 'When an official killed on order he was not guilty of murder, and if he refused an order to kill he was guilty of treason. Never was Augustine more Roman, for to allow disobedience to an unjust command would give free vent to the individual passions he so ardently condemned. Rather than incur this risk, Augustine absolved the individual soldier of moral responsibility for his official actions' (Russell, op. cit., p.22).

27. Bainton, op. cit., p.110; Russell, op. cit., p.34.

28. Bainton, op. cit., p.110.

29. Russell, op. cit., pp.60f.

30. Ibid., p.84.

31. Ibid., p.119.

32. Ibid., p.156.

33. See Herbert Butterfield, *Christianity, Diplomacy and War*, Epworth Press 1962, ch.3.

34. Russell, op. cit., p.302.

35. Gordon C. Zahn, *War, Conscience and Dissent*, Geoffrey Chapman 1967, p.78.

Chapter 3 Renunciation

1. For definitions of these words see my *Words in World Religions*, SCM Press 1979.

2. S. Gopalan, *Outlines of Jainism*, Wiley Eastern Private Ltd, New Delhi 1973: 'The most predominant characteristic of Jainism is its insistence on the strict observance of the principle of non-violence' (p.159).

3. D. Bhargava, *Jaina Ethics*, Motilal Banarsides, Delhi 1968, p.114.

4. See Max Weber, *The Religion of India*, Allen and Unwin 1958; Free Press, New York 1967, chs.1–3.

5. The twelve observances of the layman are: non-violence, truthfulness, not stealing, not coveting, chastity (most usually interpreted as chastity within marriage), avoiding unnecessary travel (and so avoiding temptation), guarding against all evils, keeping specific times for meditation, imposing special periods of self-denial, spending occasional days with monks and living as a monk during such periods, giving alms in support of monks, and limiting the number of things in daily use.

6. E. Fischer and J. Jain, *Art and Ritual – 2500 Years of Jainism in India*, Sterling Publications, New Delhi 1977, p.17. Svetambara and Digambara are the two main sects in Jainism. Generally the Digambara take the more rigorous attitudes. See *Words in World Religions*, p.52.

7. Fischer and Jain, op. cit., p.17.

8. Ibid., p.17.

9. Ibid., pp.19–21.

10. The practice of self-starvation is known as *sallekhana*.

11. See Trevor Ling, *The Buddha*, Penguin Books 1976, chs.3–5.

12. Jawaharlal Nehru once commented on Buddhism that it was 'a revolt against caste, priestcraft and ritual', *Ceylon Daily News*, May 1937, quoted in T. S. Wilkinson and M. M. Thomas, *Ambedkar and the Neo-Buddhist Movement*, CLS, Madras 1972. p.9.

13. The rise of Buddhism was resisted by Hindus in India. The Hindu reaction against Buddhism consisted partly in the rise of the *bhakti* movements, supplying a strongly devotional theistic faith which Buddhists could not match; partly in the incorporation into Hinduism of philosophies similar in many respects to Buddhism; and partly, it would seem, by political opposition. The demise of Buddhism in India was finally brought about by the Islamic invasion of Eastern India at the end of the twelfth century CE.

14. See *Words in World Religions*, p.58.

15. A modern Buddhist writer comments: 'Buddhism exhorts, it does not command. It tells us, for example, that to take life is morally wrong; but it leaves us free to determine for ourselves whether the acceptance of this teaching obliges us to be a vegetarian or a conscientious objector' (Sangharakshita, in *2500 Years of Buddhism*, Government of India 1964, p.394).

16. Cf. Trevor Ling, *The Buddha*, p.149.

17. Ibid. p.169.

18. Quoted ibid., p.170.

19. Ibid., p.195.

20. Ibid., p.187 and *2500 Years of Buddhism*, p.51.

21. 'If these various ways of expounding what Ashoka meant by Dhamma are set out synoptically, it becomes clear that the item which occurs most frequently is abstention from killing' (Ling, *The Buddha*, p.196).

22. Ibid., p.195.

23. Ibid., p.196.
24. Patanjali, *Yoga Sutras*, II, 30, 31.
25. Purusha Sukta, *Rig Veda* X: 90.
26. H. G. Rawlinson, *India – A Short Cultural History*, Cresset Press 1954, p.211.
27. Nikhilananda, *Hinduism*, Allen and Unwin 1958, pp.46f.
28. *Bhagavad Gita*, 3:35.

Chapter 4 An Apostle of Non-Violence

1. Varna is a Sanskrit word meaning 'colour', but also used to refer to the broad distinction between the four main groups of Brahmins, or priests; Kshatriyas, or warriors and rulers; Vaishya, or merchants; and Shudra, or menials. The first reference to this form of social grouping is found in the *Rig Veda* (X: 90), and it is presumed to have been introduced into India by the Aryan invaders *c*.1500 BC. The later complex caste structure can, in very broad terms, be related to this fourfold division.

2. 'The Bania . . . throughout the recorded history of Gujarat have always been a byword for the observance of high-caste and vegetarian practice. Many sections of the Bania caste are also Jains who carry the avoidance of violence to living creatures to extremes' (D. F. Pocock, *Mind, Body and Wealth*, Blackwell 1973, p.77).

3. 'The outstanding impression my mother has left on my memory is that of saintliness. She was deeply religious. She would not think of taking her meals without her daily prayers. Going to Haveli – the Vaishnava temple – was one of her daily duties. . . She would take the hardest vows and keep them without flinching' (M. K. Gandhi, *An Autobiography, or The Story of My Experiments with Truth*, The Selected Works of Mahatma Gandhi (= SWMG), Vol.1, Ahmedabad 1968, p.5.

4. SWMG 1, p.47.

5. When Gandhi left Gujarat to study in England, in 1888, his mother was very concerned about his moral welfare in a strange and distant land. She was placated by the agreement of Mohandas to take three vows, administered by a Jaina monk, 'not to touch wine, women and meat' (SWMG 1, p.56).

6. After the Crimean War, 'Russia, foiled in south-eastern Europe, resumed her forward policy in Central Asia. The rapid progress of Russia towards the border of Afghanistan was a cause of alarm and anxiety to the British Government. The conquest of the Punjab and Sind had extended the British possessions up to the hills of Afghanistan, and that country alone now stood between the advanced Russian outposts and the British Empire in India' (D. N. Majumdar, T. Raychaudhari and A. Datta, *An Advanced History of India*, Macmillan 1965, p.829).

7. SWMG 1, p.7.
8. SWMG 1, p.47.
9. SWMG 1, p.10.
10. SWMG 1, p.43.

11. SWMG 1, pp.40f.

12. Ved Mehta, *Mahatma Gandhi and His Apostles*, André Deutsch 1977.

13. Ibid., p.195.

14. Mehta records an extract from a conversation he had with Dr Sushila Nayar, once Gandhi's personal physician, and later (1962–67) India's Minister of State for Health, who had been one of the young women companions of Gandhi's later years: 'There was nothing special about sleeping next to Bapu. I heard from Bapu's own lips that when he first asked Manu to sleep with him, in Noakhali, they slept under the same covers with their clothes on, and that even on the first night Manu was snoring within minutes of getting into his bed. Some time later Bapu said to her, "We may both be killed by the Muslims at any time. We must both put our purity to the ultimate test, so that we know we are offering the purest of sacrifices, and we should now both start sleeping naked" ' (op. cit., p.203).

15. 'Everything was difficult. I could not follow, let alone taking (*sic*) interest in, the professors' lectures. It was no fault of theirs. The professors in that college were regarded as first rate. But I was so raw. At the end of the first term, I returned home' (SWMG 1, p.51).

16. SWMG 1, p.52.

17. SWMG 1, p.57.

18. SWMG 1, p.87.

19. The Theosophical Society was founded in New York in 1875 by Madam Blavatsky and Colonel Olcott. Originally the Society rested upon strange claims of occult powers and contact with spiritual 'Masters' in Tibet. But Theosophy also professed admiration for all things Indian, and encouraged positive attitudes to Hinduism among Westerners (see my *Words in World Religions*, SCM Press 1979, p.142).

20. SWNG 1, p.99.

21. SWMG 1, p.99.

22. *Bhagavad Gita* 3:35.

23. W. R. Vijayakumar, in *Ambedkar and the Neo-Buddhist Movement*, ed. T. S. Wilkinson and M. M. Thomas, CLS, Madras 1972, p.12.

24. *Bhagavad Gita* 2:11–37.

25. *Bhagavad Gita*, 3:35.

26. M. K. Gandhi, *Gita – My Mother*, Pearl Publications, Bombay 1965, pp.52–4.

27. *Harijan*, 3 October 1936.

28. SWMG 1, p.101.

29. Cf. Matthew 5.44f.

30. SWMG 1, p.149.

31. SWMG 1, p.169.

32. SWMG 1, p.171.

33. See the correspondence in *The Collected Works of Mahatma Gandhi* (=CWMG), Government of India, Delhi 1958, Vol. 1. pp.90f.

34. SWMG 1, p.157.

35. SWMG 1, pp.178–85, 200–4. See also CWMG 1, pp.139–41.

36. See Chandran Devanesen, *The Making of the Mahatma*, Orient Longmans 1969, pp.261f.

37. SWMG 1, p.204.

38. SWMG 1, p.237. For correspondence between Gandhi and Tolstoy see CWMG 9, p.593, and 10, p.210.

39. Chandran Devanesen, op. cit., p.257.

40. SWMG 1, p.236.

Chapter 5   Non-Violence in South Africa

1. SWMG 1, p.219.

2. In India, the first meeting of the Indian National Congress was held in Bombay in December 1885.

3. SWMG 1, pp.230–4.

4. The Indian corps in the Boer War was composed of eight hundred free men and three hundred indentured labourers.

5. Robert A. Huttenback, *Gandhi in South Africa – British Imperialism and the Indian Question, 1860–1914*, Cornell University Press 1971, pp.162f.

6. Ibid., pp.128f.

7. SWMG 2, pp.424f.

8. SWMG 2, p.445.

9. SWMG 2, p.446.

10. *Satyagraha in South Africa*, SWMG 3, p.136.

11. Huttenback, op. cit., p.159.

12. SWMG 3, p.137.

13. SWMG 3, p.144.

14. SWMG 3, p.151.

15. SWMG 3, p.157; see also CWMG 11, pp.22f.

16. *Harijan*, 9 August 1942.

17. CWMG 6, p.509.

18. The Transvaal elected a Het Volk Ministry, led by Botha. Smuts was the Colonial Secretary in this administration (Huttenback, op. cit., p.176).

19. Huttenback, op. cit., p.179.

20. SWMG 3, p.199.

21. Huttenback, op. cit., p.200.

22. SWMG 3, p.278.

23. Street trading was not only undertaken by those whose occupation this would normally have been. Gandhi recalled the contribution of Joseph Royeppen, a Cambridge graduate and a barrister, who became a street trader in order to court imprisonment (SWMG 3, p.298).

24. SWMG 3, p.305.

25. SWMG 3, p.386.

26. SWMG 3, p.410.

27. SWMG 3, p.428.

28. SWMG 3, p.459.

Chapter 6 Non-Violence and Civil Disobedience in India

1. M. K. Gandhi, *An Autobiography*, SWMG 2, p.592.
2. SWMG   2, p.595: 'The fact that it is mostly the real orthodox Hindus who have met the daily growing expenses of the Ashram is perhaps a clear indication that untouchability is shaken to its foundations.'
3. SWMG 2, p.602.
4. SWMG 2, p.619.
5. See Judith M. Brown, *Gandhi's Rise to Power – Indian Politics 1915–1922*, Cambridge University Press 1972. Commenting on the pattern of leadership established by Gandhi at Champaran, she writes: 'Leaving aside the recognized politicians, he went into the villages dressed in the sort of clothes villagers wore, speaking the vernacular, espousing causes which concerned his rustic audience: while doing so he drew in the local business and educated men who had little interest or influence in the Congress style of politics. He acted as go-between for these different groups, mediating between two tiers of public life, and in return secured a powerful provincial following. Even though Gandhi had not in 1917 moved entirely beyond the confines of regional loyalties, Champaran did give him an all-India public reputation' (pp.78f.). Chapter 3 of this book provides a detailed account of Gandhi's activities in Champaran, Kheda and Ahmedabad.
6. Judith Brown, op. cit., pp.94ff.
7. Gandhi, *An Autobiography*, p.643.
8. Ibid., p.650.
9. Ibid., pp.655f.
10. Ibid., p.668.
11. Judith Brown, op. cit., p.163.
12. CWMG 15, pp.87f.
13. Judith Brown, op. cit., p.165.
14. CWMG 15, pp.101f.
15. Judith Brown, op. cit., p.168.
16. Ibid., p.169.
17. Ibid., pp.171–3.
18. Gandhi, *An Autobiography*, p.690.
19. Sir Michael O'Dwyer, *India as I Knew It*, Constable 1925, pp.272f., 280f.
20. General Dyer, reporting to the General Staff, Sixteenth Division, 25 August 1919: 'I fired and continued to fire till the crowd dispersed, and I considered that this is the least amount of firing which would produce the necessary moral and widespread effect that it was my duty to produce if I was to justify my action. . . It was no longer a question of merely dispersing the crowd, but one of producing a sufficient moral effect, from a military point of view, not only on those present, but more

specially throughout the Punjab. There could be no question of undue severity' (quoted Judith Brown, op. cit., p.242).

21. Gandhi, op. cit., p.698.

22. Ibid., p.699.

23. Ibid., pp.701f.

24. Lanza del Vasto, *Gandhi to Vinoba*, Rider 1956, p.23: 'When we have beaten unjust men by unjust means we shall have taken upon ourselves injustice. . . If when the English have gone, we allow the institutions by which they founded their Empire to continue, and are satisfied with putting Indians instead of the British in high places, we shall have made only a nominal revolution and have won freedom only in word.'

25. Judith Brown, op. cit., p.185.

26. Ibid., p.228.

27. Ibid., p.244.

28. *Young India*, 7 July 1920, from CWMG 18, p.13.

29. CWMG 19, pp.182f.

30. Judith Brown, op. cit., p.307.

31. See Judith Brown, op. cit., pp.309–43, for a detailed account of participation (the numbers of those who resigned honours, etc.) in the non-cooperation campaign.

32. Ved Mehta, *Mahatma Gandhi and His Apostles*, André Deutsch 1977, p.143.

33. Ibid., p.144.

34. Quoted from *Young India*, 12 July 1928, in Judith Brown, *Gandhi and Civil Disobedience*, Cambridge University Press 1977, p.32.

35. Quoted by Ved Mehta, op. cit., p.146.

36. Ibid., p.147.

37. Judith Brown, *Gandhi and Civil Disobedience*, pp.112f.

38. Ibid., p.129.

39. CWMG 48, pp.470f.

40. Letter from C. F. Andrews, St Stephen's College, Delhi, to H. G. Haig Esq., Home Member, Government of India, Simla, 4 April 1932: file no 40/II, 1932, National Archives of India.

41. Reply to C. F. Andrews, 23 April 1932. Government of India Home Dept, DOND, 3379/32 Poll (National Archives of India).

42. *The Times of India*, 2 May 1930.

43. Ibid., 6 May 1930.

44. Home Dept. Pol., 4/15/33 (National Archives of India).

45. *The Gazette of India-Extraordinary*, New Delhi, 4 January 1932, 22/57/33 Poll. (National Archives of India).

46. Quoted by Ved Mehta, op. cit., p.149.

47. *Harijan*, 30 September 1939.

48. *Harijan*, 14 October 1939.

49. Ved Mehta, op. cit., p.152.

50. Percival Griffiths, *Modern India*, Ernest Benn ⁴1965, p.97.

51. *Harijan* recorded the decision to go to Bengal in the following way:

'Early in the morning on Wednesday last, Gandhiji announced to his party an important decision. He had decided to disperse his party, detailing each member, including the ladies, to settle down in one affected village and make himself hostage of the safety and security of the Hindu minority of that village. . . He was going to bury himself in East Bengal until such time that the Hindus and Mussalmans learnt to live together in harmony and peace' (*Harijan*, 24 November 1946).

52. Quoted by Ved Mehta, op. cit., p.171.

53. Ibid., p.171.

54. *Harijan*, 1 December 1946.

55. *Harijan*, 27 July 1947.

56. *Hindustan Times*, 30 September 1947.

57. Ved Mehta, op. cit., p.175.

58. Michael Brecher, *Nehru – A Political Biography*, p.149.

Chapter 7 The Gandhian Technique of Non-Violence

1. Leo Tolstoy, *The Law of Love and the Law of Violence*, Rudolph Field, NY 1948, p.10.

2. Ibid., p.37.

3. CWMG 9, p.593.

4. See above, pp.51f.

5. *Young India*, 11 August 1920.

6. *Young India*, 20 October 1921.

7. *Young India*, 5 November 1921.

8. *Young India*, 27 October 1921.

9. See *Harijan*, 1 September 1939 and 13 April 1940.

10. *Harijan*, 1 September 1940.

11. *Harijan*, 5 May 1946.

12. Professor Stuart Nelson, 'Gandhian Concept of Non-Violence', Seminar on Non-Violence and Social Change, University of Allahabad, January/February 1971.

13. Lanza del Vasto, *Gandhi to Vinoba*, p.23.

14. M. M. Thomas, 'Basic Approaches to Power – Gandhiji, Andrews and King', *Religion and Society* 16, 3, Bangalore, September 1969.

15. M. M. Thomas, op. cit., p.16.

16. Ibid., p.24.

17. See H. J. N. Horsburgh, *Non-Violence and Aggression – A Study of Gandhi's Moral Equivalent of War*, Oxford University Press 1968, pp.55,63.

18. See H. B. Takulia, 'The Negro American's Experiments with Non-Violent Protest', in *Gandhi, Theory and Practice*, Indian Institute of Advanced Study, Simla 1969 – Report of a Seminar, 13–26 October 1968.

19. Cf. Joan V. Bondurant, *Conquest of Violence – The Gandhian Philosophy of Conflict*, Oxford University Press, Bombay 1959, pp. vi, 12: '. . . it is not necessary to subscribe either to the asceticism so char-

acteristic of Gandhi nor to his religious notions in order to understand
and to value the central contribution of his technique of non-violence
. . . Satyagraha . . . is basically an ethic-principle, the essence of which
is a social technique of action.'

20. Ibid., p.9.

21. Matt. 5.44; Rom.12.14,21.

22. Cf. I John 4.7f., 12.

Chapter 8   Martin Luther King Jr

1. See above, pp.12ff.

2. This was a view expressed to me by many people I met and
interviewed during a visit to the United States in July and August 1980,
including such disparate observers as Martin Luther King Sr and young
black graduate students at Princeton Theological Seminary.

3. The King family house at Auburn Avenue is now owned by the
Martin Luther King Jr Center for Social Change, and is open to visitors.

4. F. Schulke (ed.), *Martin Luther King Jr. A Documentary . . .
Montgomery to Memphis*, Norton, New York 1976, p.19.

5. Quoted by David L. Lewis, *Martin Luther King: A Critical Biography*, Allen Lane: The Penguin Press 1970, p.34.

6. Ibid., pp.36f.

7. Ibid., p.36.

8. Ibid., p.x.

9. Ibid., p.45.

10. Interview with Dr Harold DeWolf, Lakeland, Florida, 29 July 1980.

11. Dr Harold DeWolf.

12. Interview with George Houser, a participant in the Journey of
Reconciliation, in New York, 15 August 1980. George Houser had been
involved in civil rights activities as far back as 1942, in Chicago, and he
told me: 'My own involvement antedates Martin Luther King by fifteen
years,' and, 'One thinks of the Greensboro restaurant action, which was
a duplication of what CORE had done, what we had done hundreds of
times, but it attracted attention at that moment for a whole variety of
reasons.'

13. Martin Luther King Jr, *Stride Toward Freedom*, Gollancz 1959,
p.46.

14. Lewis, op. cit., p.51.

15. Ibid., p.53.

16. Ibid., p.56.

17. Schulke, op. cit., p.28; see also Martin Luther King. op. cit.,
pp.59f.

18. Lewis, op. cit., p.70; King, op. cit., pp.131f.

19. King, op. cit., p.78.

20. Lewis, op. cit., p.64.

21. Ibid., p.72.

22. Ibid., p.81.

23. Peter Paris, *Black Leaders in Conflict*, The Pilgrim Press, New York 1978, p.88.

24. Interview with the Revd Albert Love, SCLC, Atlanta, 14 August 1980.

25. Revd Albert Love.

26. Martin Luther King Sr told me: 'At the moment there has been so much bickering in our organization, instead of working together; they (SCLC) were too prejudiced to work with the Martin Luther King Center for Social Change. It got so bad we had to pull out, which we hate to do. . .' (Interview, Atlanta, 7 August 1980).

27. Martin Luther King Jr wrote four books: *Stride Toward Freedom* (1957), an account of the Montgomery bus-boycott; *Strength to Love* (1963), a collection of sermons; *Why We Can't Wait* (1964), a large part of which deals with the Birmingham campaign; *Chaos or Community?* (1967). Shortly after his death, a fifth book, *Trumpet of Conscience* (1968), was published, giving the texts of a series of broadcast talks.

28. Lewis, op. cit., p.99.

29. Ibid., p.105.

Chapter 9 Non-Violence or Black Power?

1. Lewis, *Martin Luther King*, p.116.

2. Ibid., pp.121f.

3. Schulke, *Martin Luther King Jr*, p.39.

4. Interview with Revd Ed Brown, Atlanta, 13 August 1980.

5. Lewis, op. cit., pp.125–9.

6. Lewis, op. cit., p.129.

7. See above, pp.96ff.

8. Schulke, op. cit., p.40.

9. Schulke, op. cit., p.42; Lewis, op. cit., p.132.

10. Schulke, op. cit., p.44.

11. Lewis, op. cit., p.151.

12. Peter J. Paris, *Black Leaders in Conflict*, p.26.

13. Ibid., p.25.

14. William Robert Miller, *Martin Luther King Jr: His Life, Martyrdom and Meaning for the World*, Weybright, New York 1968, p.137.

15. David J. Garrow, *Protest at Selma – Martin Luther King Jr and the Voting Rights Act of 1965*, Yale University Press 1978, pp.2ff.

16. Dr Eugene Carson Blake told me how he was drawn into the civil rights movement: 'I saw the hoses and police dogs in Birmingham on TV in May of 1963 and got converted' (Interview, Stamford, Connecticut, 26 July 1980).

17. Schulke, op. cit., p.71.

18. Lewis, op. cit., p.180.

19. Martin Luther King Jr, *Why We Can't Wait*, Harper and Row, New York 1964, p.61. The full commandments printed on the Commitment Cards read:

Meditate daily on the teachings and life of Jesus.

Remember always that the nonviolent movement in Birmingham seeks justice and reconciliation, not victory.

Walk and talk in the manner of love, for God is love.

Pray daily to be used by God in order that all men might be free.

Sacrifice personal wishes in order that all men might be free.

Observe with both friend and foe the ordinary rules of courtesy.

Seek to perform regular service for others, and for the world.

Refrain from the violence of fist, tongue, or heart.

Strive to be in good spiritual and bodily health.

Follow the directions of the movement and of the captain on a demonstration.

20. Ibid., pp.77–100.

21. On 20 May the Supreme Court ruled that Birmingham's segregation laws were unconstitutional.

22. Ibid., pp.112f.

23. Lewis, op. cit., p.208.

24. Interview with Dr Eugene Carson Blake, Stamford, Connecticut, 26 July 1980.

25. Lewis, op. cit., p.221.

26. The full speech is in Schulke, op. cit., p.218.

27. Lewis, op. cit., p.221.

28. Garrow, op. cit., pp.15–17.

29. James C. Harvey, *Black Civil Rights during the Johnson Administration*, University and College Press of Mississippi, 1973, p.157.

30. Ibid., p.29.

31. Ibid., p.29.

32. Ibid., p.28.

33. Schulke, op. cit., p.133.

34. Ibid., p.137.

35. Ibid., pp.140f.

36. Lewis, op. cit., p.275.

37. Accounts of the number involved in the second march vary. Schulke records 1500 (p.146); Lewis gives the total as 3000 (p.281).

38. Quoted by Lewis, op. cit., p.279.

39. Lewis, op. cit., p.281.

40. Lewis, op. cit., pp.281f.

41. Kenneth B. Clark (ed.), *The Negro Protest*, pp.26f., quoted in Peter J. Paris, op. cit., pp.152f.

42. Breitman, *Malcolm X Speaks*, p.26, quoted in Peter J. Paris, op. cit., p.170.

43. Lewis, op. cit., p.292.

44. See David J. Garrow, op. cit., ch.4.

45. James C. Harvey, op. cit., p.33.

46. Harvey, op. cit., p.31.

47. Harvey, op. cit., p.34f.

48. Schulke, op. cit., p.176.

49. Quoted in Lewis, op. cit., p.325.

50. Martin Luther King Jr, *Chaos or Community?*, Hodder and Stoughton 1967, p.27.

51. Ibid., p.5.

52. Ibid., p.145.

53. Lewis, op. cit., p.296.

54. Interview with the Revd Albert E. Love, Southern Christian Leadership Conference, Atlanta, 14 August 1980.

55. Martin Luther King Jr, *Chaos or Community?*, p.35.

56. See Jane Rockman (ed.), *Peace in Search of Makers*, Judson Press, Valley Forge 1979.

57. Lewis, op. cit., p.360.

58. Ibid., p.361.

59. Ibid., p.360.

60. Ibid., p.387.

61. For an analysis of the motives and character of James Earl Ray, see William Bradford Huie, *He Slew the Dreamer*, W. H. Allen 1970.

62. From a copy of the original text of the Funeral Tribute, given to me by Dr Harold DeWolf.

Chapter 10 Martin Luther King's Understanding of Gandhian Non-Violence

1. See above, p.125.

2. Interview, Atlanta, 7 August 1980.

3. Interview, Lakeland, Florida, 29 July 1980.

4. Martin Ceadel, *Pacifism in Britain 1914–1945 – The Defining of a Faith*, Clarendon Press 1980, p.3.

5. Ibid., p.5.

6. Barrie Paskins and Michael Dockrill, *The Ethics of War*, Duckworth 1979, p.112.

7. Martin Luther King Jr, *Stride Toward Freedom*, p.85.

8. Ibid., pp.90f.

9. William Robert Miller, *Martin Luther King Jr – His Life, Martyrdom and Meaning for the World*, p.19.

10. A view first expressed in *Moral Man and Immoral Society*, Scribner, New York 1932 and SCM Press 1963.

11. *Stride Toward Freedom*, p.92.

12. Ibid., p.93.

13. W. R. Miller, op. cit., p.22. In a footnote Miller adds: 'In fairness to Reinhold Niebuhr, it should be pointed out that his views over the years have been broader than those of this interpreters, pro and con. At various times, he endorsed the use of violence in labour struggles while holding firmly to nonviolence in international affairs, later urged armed resistance to fascism, went on to commend King's followers for their blend of perfectionism and realism, and most recently strove to end the war in Vietnam.'

14. The first form of the 'Essay on Civil Disobedience' was a lecture delivered at Concord Lyceum in 1848. In 1849 it was published in Elizabeth Peabody's *Aesthetic Papers*, but largely ignored until after Thoreau's death. In 1903 it appeared by itself in England in a cheap paperback edition.

15. *Stride Toward Freedom*, p.85.

16. Martin King does not appear to refer to the fourth Greek word for love, *storge*, or natural affection. For a full discussion of the concept of agape see A. Nygren, *Agape and Eros*, SPCK 1957.

17. I Cor. 13.4–6.

18. *Stride Toward Freedom*, p.85.

19. Ibid., p.60

20. Ibid., p.60.

21. Ibid., p.78.

22. Ibid., pp.78f.

23. Ibid., p.81.

24. See above, p.15.

25. W. R. Miller in *Gandhi Marg* 49, 1969, quoted by M. M. Thomas, 'Basic Approaches to Power – Gandhiji, Andrews and King', *Religion and Society* XVI, 3, September 1969.

26. M. M. Thomas, op. cit., p.23.

27. Martin Luther King Jr, *Chaos or Community?*, Hodder and Stoughton 1967, p.37.

28. *Stride Toward Freedom*, p.96.

29. Ibid., p.96.

30. Ibid., p.96.

31. Ibid., p.100.

32. In a series of broadcast talks in November and December 1967, less than six months before his death, Martin King spoke about his opposition to the Vietnam War: 'Negroes are conscripted in double measure for combat. They constitute more than 20 per cent of the front-line troops in a war of unprecedented savagery, although their proportion in the population is 10 per cent. They are marching under slogans of democracy, to defend a Saigon government that scorns democracy. At home they know there is no genuine democracy for their people, and on their return they will be restored to a grim life as second-class citizens even if they are bedecked with heroes' medals' (*The Trumpet of Conscience*, Hodder and Stoughton 1968, p.19). In another talk in the series, he gave three reasons for opposing Vietnam: 1. Because it drained funds that might otherwise have been devoted to the Poverty Programme to help blacks. 2. Because a higher proportion of blacks than whites are being sent to die. 3. Because encouraging negroes to be violent in Vietnam undermined his appeals to them for non-violence in the USA (ibid, pp.30f.).

33. Interview with Dr Harold DeWolf, Tampa, Florida, 29 July 1980.

34. *Why We Can't Wait*, Harper and Row, New York 1964, p.169.

35. *Strength to Love* (Harper and Row 1963), Hodder and Stoughton 1964, p.140.

36. Ibid., p.140.

37. See above, p.139.

38. M. M. Thomas, op. cit., p.25.

Chapter 11   A Technique for Loving – The Possibilities
for Non-Violence

1. The response to the ethical questions was not always encouraging. So Giulio Douhet wrote in *The Command of the Air*, New York 1942: 'War will always be inhuman, and the means which are used in it cannot be classified as acceptable or not acceptable except according to their efficacy, potentiality, or harmfulness to the enemy' (quoted in Barrie Paskins and Michael Dockrill, *The Ethics of War*, Duckworth 1979, p.10).

2. Paskins and Dockrill, op. cit., p.24.

3. Ibid., p.42.

4. N. Frankland, *Bomber Offensive: The Devastation of Europe*, New York 1970, pp.38f. Quoted in Michael Walzer, *Just and Unjust Wars*, Allen Lane: The Penguin Press 1978, p.258.

5. C. Webster and N. Frankland, *The Strategic Air Offensive Against Germany, 1939–1945*, London 1961 (four vols), quoted in Paskins and Dockrill, op. cit., pp.29f.

6. Paskins and Dockrill, op. cit., p.30.

7. M. Walzer, *Just and Unjust Wars*, p.256.

8. Paskins and Dockrill, op. cit., p.28.

9. Ibid., p.41.

10. Ibid., p.39.

11. Ibid., pp.42–8.

12. Walzer, op. cit., p.255.

13. See Paskins and Dockrill, op. cit., p.52.

14. Ibid., p.52.

15. In *The Irreversible Decision 1939–1950*, New York 1961, quoted in Paskins and Dockrill, op. cit., pp.54f.

16. Paskins and Dockrill, op. cit., p.57.

17. Walzer, op. cit., p.268.

18. M. Walzer, 'World War II: Why This War Was Different', in *War and Moral Responsibility*, ed. R. B. Brandt et al., Princeton University Press 1974.

19. Paskins and Dockrill, op. cit., p.276.

20. See G. E. M. Anscombe, 'War and Murder', in *Nuclear Weapons and Christian Conscience*, ed. Walter Stein, Burns and Oates 1963.

21. Walzer, *Just and Unjust Wars*, p.324.

22. Walzer, ibid., p.272.

23. Paskins and Dockrill, op. cit., p.62.

24. Richard J. Barnet, 'History of the Arms Race 1945–1978', in *Peace in Search of Makers*, Judson Press, Valley Forge 1979.

25. T. M. Taylor and R. S. Bilheimer, *Christians and the Prevention of War in an Atomic Age*, SCM Press 1961.

26. *Non-Violent Action, A Report produced by the United Reformed Church*, SCM Press 1973, p.8.

27. Paul Ramsey, *The Just War: Force and Political Responsibility*, Scribner, New York 1968.

28. Richard Greenwood, 'Labor, Unemployment and Arms', in *Peace in Search of Makers*, p.26.

29. George Wald, 'Nuclear War is Thinkable and Possible', in *Peace in Search of Makers*, p.74.

30. *Non-Violent Action*, p.8.

31. Walzer, op. cit., p.330.

32. Ibid., p.331.

33. See above, pp.139ff.

34. Paskins and Dockrill, op. cit., p.260.

35. Ibid., p.261.

Index